Praise for *After Jail, Before Freedom*

"'It is a rough intersection between the writing and the living,' David Coogan writes in *After Jail, Before Freedom,* and the brilliant book that follows proves that adage many times over. Following five men—Kelvin, Dean, Ronald, Naji, and Stan—released from prison to navigate the treacherous terrain of reentry and tell their stories in their own unflinching voices, the book also interweaves Coogan's own reckoning with what it means to witness someone else's freedom, to be complicit in both the successes and the failures, even in the act of writing and publishing a memoir. These coauthors reveal what the system doesn't prepare you for: The stigma of a felony conviction; the struggle to find a job, battle addiction, and be a father; and how, after release, trauma won't ever let you go. Changing your life means fighting for it every single day. This is a story about redemption, resilience, and the courage it takes to build a new life from the wreckage of the old. What Coogan does most masterfully is lay bare his own complicity—and all of ours—in the very struggle he documents so potently and poignantly. We have plenty of writing about what happens inside a prison; this crucial book tells us what happens after."

—Ravi Shankar, Pushcart Prize-winning author of *Correctional*

"*After Jail, Before Freedom* is comparable to the classic sociological study of street corner Black men, *Tally's Corner* by Elliot Liebow. Both shed light and expose the hidden stories of invisible people in America. David Coogan, as author, writing instructor, mentor, witness, helper, navigator, and participant observer, tells and shares the stories of five men in their reentry and reintegration process after prison. This is nonfiction that is a must-read as modern American prison writing. Coogan illuminates the words of five formerly incarcerated men and creates a powerful and lasting narrative as an example of the American prison memoir. *After Jail, Before Freedom* is a fabulous and innovative project that reflects how important American prison writing has become in America."

—Flores Forbes, author of *Invisible Men: A Contemporary Slave Narrative in the Era of Mass Incarceration*

"An intimate and powerful look into the realities of reentry that reintroduces us to five men we first met while they were still in jail. After years in prison, we see the many obstacles they face and the triumphs they earn, a microcosm of an experience hundreds of thousands face every year. David Coogan once again helps open a door into the system of mass incarceration, and helps those in it speak for themselves. A must-read if you want to hear it real and unfiltered."

—Kenneth Hartman, award-winning author of
Mother California: A Story of Redemption Behind Bars

"This powerful series of essays by Dave Coogan and his former jail students helps to fill in a vital gap in the growing literature emerging from both legalized human caging and the later-life memoirs of people living beyond incarceration. This is the gap between jail gates and the first precarious or crumbling footholds in a world that won't stop punishing the formerly incarcerated—for their youthful reaction to trauma, their unequal opportunities, their race, and their poverty. Kelvin Belton, Stanley Craddock, Ronald Fountain, Naji Mujahid, and Dean Turner offer the perspicacity, profound self-reflection, and self-awareness—in inviting prose style—they have gained from being fed into the machinery of the US criminal-legal system. Here they emerge to make clear to readers that their hearts and resilience have survived this system that wants to break people, that they *will not* be counted among the broken. This is important reading for anyone committed to understanding the human toll of incarceration in the US today."

—Doran Larson, founder and co-director of The
American Prison Writing Archive (prisonwitness.org)

AFTER JAIL, BEFORE FREEDOM

David Coogan

with

Kelvin Belton

Stanley Craddock

Ronald Fountain

Naji Mujahid

Dean Turner

ISBN (Paperback): 978-1-966369-05-9
Library of Congress Control Number: 2026907069

Front cover photo courtesy of John Dooley
Author photos courtesy of Skip Rowland
Designed by Sami Langston
Project managed by Haley Simpkiss

Published by
Brandylane Publishers, Inc.
5 S. 1st Street
Richmond, Virginia 23219

brandylanepublishers.com

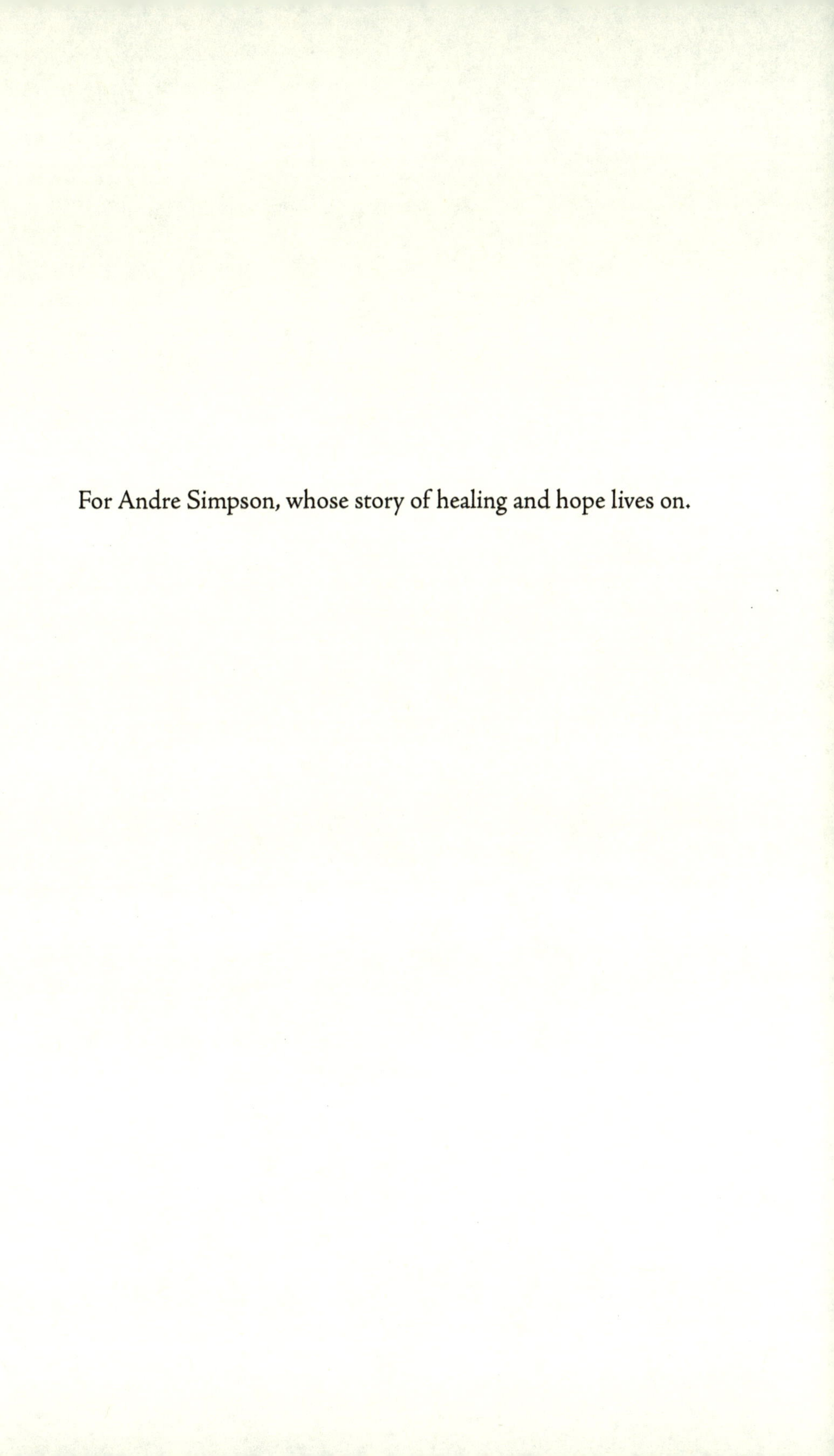

For Andre Simpson, whose story of healing and hope lives on.

Contents

Acknowledgements

I want to thank my coauthors, Kelvin Belton, Stan Craddock, Ron Fountain, Naji Mujahid, and Dean Turner, for sharing their lives with me over these many years. Without our brotherhood, there would be no book. Thanks also to the many students, friends, and family members who listened to my stories that formed the basis of these essays, especially my daughter, Lucy, who heard many of my first drafts. Further thanks go to Liz Canfield, Laura Coates, Sonja Livingston, Jessica Hendry Nelson, Larry Palmer, and Margaret Wardlaw for their insightful feedback on my writing, and to Tamurlaine Melby for her expert editing of the manuscript. Finally, I would like to acknowledge the College of Humanities and Sciences at Virginia Commonwealth University for providing me with research leave to complete this manuscript.

Introduction

A few months after I moved to Richmond to start my new job as an assistant professor of English, I started a memoir writing class at the city jail. I had never been to a jail before or known anyone who had gone. But after a violent crime took place in my new neighborhood, I began to wonder about people whose lives unwind in such a way that engaging in crime seemed plausible, maybe even inevitable. Did they know how that story had formed? Could they figure it out by writing the story down? And could writing about their lives help them change direction and stay out of jail?

A core group formed in the summer of 2006 to develop the vision: Kelvin Belton, Stanley Craddock, Ronald Fountain, Naji Mujahid, Andre Simpson, and Dean Turner. I had only planned on teaching the course over the summer. I ended up staying nine months. When the last of that core group was shipped to prison in the spring of 2007, I kept the class going in letters. Four more people joined the project from prison as letter writers: Karl Black, Bradley Greene, Tony Martin, and Terence Scruggs. We resolved to make a book of our writings.

Then they began to get out. Not all at once, but one at a time. And when they got out, they came to see me. Between 2007 and 2015, my little office at Virginia Commonwealth University was an unofficial stop on their way home from the Virginia Department of Corrections. I was unprepared for what happened next.

When they were incarcerated, I saw them through their writing, and myself through the teaching. Writing showed me how they had gotten trapped in patterns that revealed their character developing over time. Writing led to greater awareness of—and compassion for—the person who had struggled earlier in life but who now chose to struggle differently. When they got out, I realized, dimly, that they were done writing. I was done teaching. Nothing lay between us but reality unfolding.

It is a rough intersection between the writing and the living. An endless hiss of traffic. A relentless dare. Approaching these intersections with them felt like that dream where the mind says run, but all the body does is quiver. I could not cross these streets in their lives any more than I could move their legs. I could offer encouragement and advice—and sometimes I tried to do more—but ultimately, I was a witness to what they had to do.

What did they have to do? And how would I know when they had done it? External changes—a new job, a new car—were important but did not necessarily add up to anything. Internal shifts were, by definition, inaccessible to me. I could speculate. I could ask. But how would I know when they had arrived in the clearing of their new lives? Eventually, I came to realize that there was no arriving. There was no "out" in writing your way out. There was only the active imagination of it, a reaching for change in the living, the same as in the writing. When I began working from that insight, I understood at last that watching them had become a way of watching myself. Seeing them struggle to change their lives was changing how I saw life.

When they worried about finding a job and making money, I realized how little I thought about money. (I had a job. I was earning money.) When they worried about getting to that job without a car, I simply drove. More than once, I was at home when one of the guys called to tell me he was homeless. My middle-classness often made me myopic. So, too, my whiteness. These were the glasses I had been wearing so long I often forgot they were even on my head. I had to learn how to see without them. More than once, I failed to read the tea leaves in their situations for signs of frustration, depression, or relapse. How was I supposed to know when to pick up that cup and study what was inside?

While I was getting my bearings in this new role as witness, resource, ally, and mentor, we published *Writing Our Way Out: Memoirs from Jail* (2015). In it, I tell the story of the writing class, and they tell their life stories, beginning with their earliest memories of the past, the problems they ran into, the punishments they received, and their sense of life's possibilities. The story begins in 2006 in jail and ends in 2010, when all but Stan had been released from prison.

After Jail, Before Freedom picks up the story where *Writing Our Way Out* ends. It follows them in reentry as they contend with the stigma of a felony conviction, racial discrimination, unstable living conditions, lousy job situations, the allure of addiction, enduring trauma, and ongoing problems with the criminal justice system. The book is arranged chronologically and collaboratively to tell a story whose sum is greater than its parts. All of the surviving authors of *Writing Our Way Out* were invited to contribute. Of those men, Dean, Ronald, Stan, Naji, and Kelvin chose to write again. Their chapters intertwine with mine.

What we share is true to the best of our recollections. We have changed the names of some people to protect their privacy. As I did with the first book, I worked with each man to lightly edit his writing to match the sound of his voice with the conventions of standard, edited English. Everyone has given permission for the way their work appears here.

The jail where I met these guys—the one on the cover of this book—is gone. It was razed in 2014 and replaced with a new jail. But when I think about the writing class that started me on this journey, I think about the cinder block chapel in the old Richmond City Jail.

When those Saturday sessions ended in the spring of 2007, I felt a strange longing for the jail. I wanted to return to start another writing class, but I was too busy meeting with the guys and working on *Writing Our Way Out* to do so. To fill the gap, I began reading the work of other Americans who had been to prison. When I looked up a year later, I had enough material for a college course.

In 2008, I created that course in prison literature. In addition to assigned readings, the students also read the draft memoirs by the guys. When the guys got out of jail, they came to campus to visit this class. Something sparked when my students could connect the guys' stories with their own lives. Something sparked in the guys, too, as they shared with people sympathetic to their stories. I vowed not to let those sparks die.

In 2011, I went back to the jail to teach a new writing course based on the one in *Writing Our Way Out*. And I invited other professors in the humanities to design their own courses for Open Minds—a college program I created at the jail offering dual enrollment courses for residents of the jail and students at Virginia Commonwealth University (VCU). In addition to my writing course, we now had courses in gender studies, Zen Buddhism, and African American literature. It became a regular part of the semester for some of us to leave campus with our students and go have class with the residents at the jail.

While I was pleased to be teaching in the jail again, I was no more convinced that jails worked than when I began teaching there five years prior.

Why did people have to experience incarceration in order to get education? With that question in mind, I partnered with the Richmond Commonwealth Attorney's Office in 2018 to divert low-level offenders away from court to campus to take the same writing course I was teaching for Open Minds. There, they joined VCU students to write about their lives and share what they knew about life. *Writing Our Way Out* became the class text. And some of my coauthors became their writing coaches.

Normally, when a class ends, the students leave the room. When the class at the jail ended in 2007, I followed Stan, Dean, Kelvin, Ron, and Naji into the rooms of their lives. The world that they knew before jail was still there. It had not changed. But they were determined to make a change. This book tells the story of what happened when they tried.

1
Sacred Ground

Dave

Fall, 2007. The steakhouse was more or less what I expected. Dim lighting, dark wainscotting, brittle air conditioning. The bartender wore a white collared shirt and a black vest. The hostess stood behind a podium with her hair pulled back from her face. She looked like a college student.

"Table for one?"

"Oh, thanks, no, I'm just here to see Dean." Her mood dipped. Her face squished.

"How do you know *Dean?*" She couldn't understand how a guy in the lobby knew the guy back there working. I was about to explain. I could feel the words forming: about the writing class at the jail where I met Dean, about the book we were making. Then it hit me. I was not on campus talking to a student. Dean was not in jail. He was somewhere in this steakhouse. I didn't know what he had revealed to get the job, or what the hostess knew about his past. If I told her the truth, she could gossip with the bartender, who might tell the manager, who might want to fire Dean. Even if that was unlikely, the news that he had been to prison could make her uncomfortable. There was no speaking with impunity.

"He's just a friend," I said. "I'm just here to say hi and give him this." I held up a manila envelope stuffed with his writing. She offered to give it to him for me. I offered to come back another time. She waffled. I sensed her weighing the risks of leaving the podium.

"It's okay," I said and turned to leave.

"Hold on." She darted back to the kitchen.

I heard him before I saw him. "Ha-ha! What's up, Dave! Whatchu doing?" He wore kitchen whites, a black skull cap, and a boisterous grin.

"Just on my way home from campus. Thought I'd stop in to say hey."

"Okay, yeah, that's what's up!"

"And I got this for you. It's that last piece you wrote for the book. I typed it up. I wanted you to check out the edits." The hostess leaned on the podium, pretending not to listen.

"Oh, okay, okay. I can do that. I'll do it tomorrow when I'm off." We dapped. Then I turned to leave. I could sense the eyes of the hostess on my back as I pushed open the door.

The sun warmed my face as I made my way across the cobblestones, away from the steakhouse and the James River behind it. Along with the old brick buildings, the cobblestones made Shockoe Bottom feel quaint. It was not always that way, I later learned. The whole area had once been paved over. In the 1970s, civic groups looking to boost tourism took up the asphalt,[1] and this little part of Shockoe Bottom, known as Shockoe Slip, became a magnet for fine restaurants, shops, and hotels.

Historical tourism depends upon a narrative and the images it evokes. I don't know what the civic groups had imagined, but I'm guessing it was horses and carriages, ladies in hoop skirts, and bearded men in dark suits conferring. Not Africans in coffles, auction blocks, the nearby jail for enslaved people, and their burial ground. Shockoe Bottom was once the largest marketplace for enslaved people outside of New Orleans. I had no idea. At the time, there were no historical markers telling the story. Before activists reclaimed the burial ground for history in 2011, it was a parking lot owned by my university.

After the Civil War, when the enslaved people had been freed, the Union Army returned control of Richmond to the Confederates, who issued a pass system for moving about the city. Over eight hundred freed people looking for their relatives or looking for jobs were arrested for not having a pass during the first two weeks under the new system.[2] The historian and Episcopalian priest Ben Campbell writes that the vagrancy law worked hand in glove with the economy at the time, noting that "in many Virginia localities white employers had already made agreements not to hire freedmen at normal wages, thus forcing wages to be depressed and providing an opportunity for the enforcement of the vagrancy statute."[3] The war was over. But the Thirteenth Amendment allowed slavery as a punishment for those convicted of a crime.

I crossed through the 17th Street farmers market by the train station, whose parking lot sits near a grassy plot of land that marks the site of Lumpkin's Jail, a nineteenth-century slave jail and trading complex that was notorious for the cruelty of its owner. Low brick buildings face an open square for vendors or bands to set up. Today, those buildings house bars and restaurants. In the years before the Civil War, there were hotels and meeting rooms with auction blocks and enslaved people drawn from Lumpkin's Jail for the sale. The city had proposed building a minor league baseball stadium here in 2005.[4] Baseball, the mayor and his people claimed, would boost tourism. Activists found the idea of a baseball stadium covering over the history of slavery crass. They argued that the city should instead build a museum to honor the memory and contributions of enslaved people. Proponents of the stadium found the idea of a museum to slavery depressing. The city entered into a stasis.

Slavery did not end after the Civil War, writes Christina Sharpe in her book, *In the Wake: On Blackness and Being*. It merely changed forms. This poses a conundrum in reality and in history, Sharpe says: "How do we memorialize an event that is still ongoing?" What do we curate? Where do we assemble? She continues with another difficult question: "Might we instead understand the absence of a National Slavery Museum in the United States as recognition of the ongoingness of the conditions of capture?"[5]

The parallels are not precise. Still, they haunted me. Dean had been freed from jail but was struggling to get enough hours at the steakhouse to pay his bills. He could get another job to supplement his income. He could lie on the application when they asked if he had a felony conviction. He could tell the truth and risk not getting the job. Or he could go back to selling drugs, risk getting caught, and go back to jail.

These days, the entrance to the African Burial Ground is easy to miss. You have to walk away from the site of Lumpkin's Jail up Broad Street toward the entrance ramp for the highway until you see a stone stairwell that takes you down under the overpass. Young grass covers the remains of the enslaved. Cars and trucks whir overhead. Signs prohibit recreational activities. Placards tell a story of what once took place here. At the time of this writing, there is still no museum to slavery in Shockoe Bottom. But they did build a new jail—what they call the Richmond City Justice Center—on the site of the old Richmond City Jail, a mile away from where Lumpkin's Jail once stood.

2
Decent Money

Dean

When I got out of jail in 2007, I was going through life kind of easy as can be. Normal life to a certain extent because I kept my pain bottled up, hidden from my family and friends. Not quite as much as before, but back then, when I was a kid, behind closed doors, I was getting abused. A young, single, Black mother. Well, not single, because she was married to my stepfather, who was a mail carrier for the United States Postal Service. He treated me like his own son. He helped me with my homework, took me to baseball games, football games, the movies, bought me clothes, and came to all of my big events: basketball and football games, and graduations. He did more for me than my real dad ever did, but we're not going to mention him. This is a new beginning.

It's 2007. My youngest daughter just turned one year old, and I'm finally going to have a chance to hold her, kiss her, love on her, and protect her. It's a great feeling, but first I must go get this job that my cousin lined me up with while I was in jail. Boy, was I happy I didn't have to come back out into society and beat the pavement down for weeks at a time trying to impress someone who really doesn't give two fucks about you.

The job he got me was at Morton's Steakhouse as a dishwasher, making decent money. I love the atmosphere and my coworkers. It's a lot different for me here. Everyone is so cool and friendly. My supervisor is from Africa, and boy, can he cook! He can throw down. I used to sit back and watch how he went about his day-to-day operation. It made me curious. I used to say to myself, "This doesn't look too hard. I can do this." So, I started asking questions every once in a while. I guess he saw the look in my eye. That's when he began to call me over to watch him put a few dishes together. He would point out a couple of things and ask me did I have any questions. He told me to read the ingredients, make sure I mastered that part, then he wanted to get the timing down, measurements down, and seasoning down pat. He told me everything else is self-explanatory. The rest is on me. Put your finishing touch on it. And that's exactly what I did.

I started practicing with small dishes that I could handle. I didn't want to burn up my grandmother's kitchen. She would kill me! So I began with the bacon, fried apples, and eggs with cheese. My first try, I burned the pancakes, the home fries, and the apples. It was so funny. My grandmother had me all hyped up, talking about how it smells so delicious. You know I'm gassed when I brought her that plate. But the expression on her face told the story. My confidence went right out the window with the smell. I was devastated, crushed!

But, you know, Grandmother said, "Deanie, don't worry about a damn thing. I couldn't cook a lick when I met your grandfather." We laughed.

"For real, Grandma?" I thought she was just trying to make me feel good, but later my mother told me the same thing. My grandfather could cook his ass off, and he taught my grandmother.

My grandmother was something else. She was a tough woman. She told me to never give up on my dreams, and she never gave up on me. She was a fighter. She always found a way to make it work. I think about her all the time. She was special, humble, smart, and persevered through anything—a strong Black woman who kept her family together.

"One day I'm going to make you proud of me," I told her.

"I've always been proud of you. You're my pride and joy, my first grand, and my birthday present."

I didn't stop at burnt breakfast. I worked diligently to master my craft, reading recipes, watching videos on YouTube to see how different chefs do things. It's been a journey, but now I have the confidence to go into a kitchen and put something delicious together for people. My dream is to finally get a food truck so I can spread the love to other people and make an honest living.

I worked at Morton's Steakhouse for about a year. Then I went for job number two. I got hired on with Food Lion, where I worked in three different departments: dairy, produce, and dry foods. So, I was working two jobs. I was chasing after the bag, going hard in the paint, but the whole time, the streets were calling me, whispering my nickname: *Boogie. Boogie.* I'm trying to ignore it. The more time I spend away from the streets, the better I am. But the devil is always working, and he's the master of illusions. A lot of buffoonery.

* * *

Let me take you back to the '90s when things weren't so hard for a brother. That's when I came back to Virginia. I was twenty-seven. I was looking for an opportunity to make a better living. Plus, my money had run out. I was in NYC struggling to get by, and it wasn't a good feeling. So, I reached out to a couple of homies of mine. I needed to get back on my feet and fast. I paged Tee and Skully all morning because I was done with NYC. I couldn't find a decent-paying job. The one I had wasn't giving me enough hours to get ahead in life. Plus, I can't front: I was missing Virginia a little. Around 2 p.m., Tee finally decided to hit me back.

"Yo, Boogie, what's really good, Daddio?"

"Shit, my niggah, I'm kinda fucked up in the game. I'm trying to get back on my feet. I wanna come back down there, but I'm not fucking with Petersburg. Can you plug me in?"

"Yo, you already know I gotcha."

"Word!"

"I got the crazy connect. We can eat off the same plate of food. Where are you going to rest your head at?"

"Shit, I'm good." My grandmother was living in Richmond. I was betting she would love to have me back in Virginia. I was going to have to work—find a job. She ain't going for me straight hustling. It had to be something positive. After my conversation with Tee, I called my grandmother to ask if I could come back to Richmond. She didn't hesitate. She said yes, I could. Boy, was I happy!

It took me close to a week to get all my stuff together. I spoke to my connect. He threw me a six deuce, which is 62 grams of coke. I jumped on Amtrak, and I was heading back to Virginia.

Once I was back in Richmond, I decided to take a few days to relax and get some sunshine and fresh air. I walked around the neighborhood. My grandmother loved living in the Southside of Richmond, the Forest Hill section. I took it as a very uppity white neighborhood, but it was also mixed with Black, so a little of both. On one side, it was clean, nice, beautiful homes, over by Forest Hill Park. The Westover Hills section wasn't too bad either. They had a one-dollar movie theater. A couple of game rooms where

I could shoot pool or play ping pong. I love tabletop games, but I was still balling, so I was definitely looking for some basketball courts so I could cut some ass. We used to ball all day and night. I'm talking full court, too, in the blazing sun, but we were young. Nobody was worried about getting heat stroke or anything like that. I think we were into every sport. Just imagine growing up in Harlem. There's so much you can get into. It's ridiculous. Softball, basketball, and football, we played them all. But the main thing is you'd better know how to fight. You can't be a pussy.

After a few days in Richmond, I was back on my grind, back in my paper chase mode, but I was also working temp jobs because I couldn't find a decent-paying job. Everything in the city at this time was paying slave wages. The bare minimum. So, you know, I couldn't rock with that for too much longer, as the jobs became unbearable.

I started easing back into the game, selling drugs. Tee, Scully, and I were all over Richmond. Northside. Southside. Church Hill. Newtown. Highland Park. You know what was crazy about the whole thing? My grandmother and my mom were going back to school. All this time I've been around my grandmother, I never knew she didn't finish high school, but she never let that stop her from accomplishing what she wanted in life. She always had a job. She always had her own place. She always dressed nice. And I never saw her cry or complain about her situation. She never stopped fighting. She was my hero and my inspiration. She always found a way to make it, no matter the circumstances. I think that's where I get my toughness from—her, my mother, my aunt Toni, and my OGs. They say it takes a village to raise a child.

Aight! Like I said before, I'm on my hustle, chasing after a dollar, not a care in the world. Not thinking about consequences or my future. I'm living in the now, which would be my downfall because I should have been a little smarter with my moves, with my lifestyle, with everything. But I was caught up in the moment.

Hip-hop was taking off—Bad Boy Records, Death Row Records, No Limit, Def Jam. Shit was moving on a bigger scale. Money was coming in at a faster pace. Then I get offered a job as head of A&R with an up-and-coming record label out of Richmond called PROBIZ. The guy started his company selling T-shirts. Then he decided to branch off into the modeling industry and then the music industry. Since one of my homies at the time was signed to him, he decided to pull me in so we could all eat. Plus, I knew a lot of people already working in the music industry.

Now, not only am I getting money hustling, but I'm also getting legit money from a real, paying job that I like. I get to travel and meet new talent. I get to sign artists, travel for free, and go to exclusive parties and concerts for free. In my mind, I think it's the coolest thing rocking for me, but in reality, it was turning me into a monster. You couldn't tell me shit. I was that niggah. I was getting money, sleeping with plenty of women in different cities and states. I'm driving now, dressing fly as shit. That's what we Harlem kats do! I'm on top of the world. So I thought. But God always finds a way to humble your ass when you're trying to do it the easy and fast way. That's exactly what He did. He took back almost everything He gave me.

Anyway, while I was out of town, on semi-vacation, my connect called me and told me to be careful, clean up the crib, because we had a leak somewhere. The police must have been watching my place. I called my girl and told her to go by my house. She went to the crib and removed all the weed. That still didn't work. In the midst of my coming back home to get more money and fresh clothes, the police raided my home. I barely had anything they could use for a real case against me—except for the gun. Damn! I forgot all about the firearm, which became the smoking gun that got me convicted. I retained one of the best attorneys in Richmond, but to no avail. They gave me the least amount of time you could get back then: two years.

* * *

As I get a little older and wiser, I start to understand my weaknesses, my triggers. I know that I can't be around certain people, places, and things. I can't feel trapped or that my back is against the wall, because that's when I go into survival mode. And that's when the Harlem in me comes out, and I'm all in. I've got to get it, like Malcolm X said, "by any means necessary." Well, to a certain extent. We ain't out there hurting anyone, killing anyone, robbing people of their hard-earned money, but we are going hard in the paint, meaning I'm going to sell as much weed or crack as people want to buy and smoke.

I know, I know. I'm destroying my own community, but when I'm in that state of mind, it's survival of the fittest, and fuck you if you're not on my team. My mind is focused on one thing, and that's climbing out of this hole I'm in, making sure I stay afloat. It's rough in these streets, but sometimes the wounds are self-inflicted. If we stay the course, stay on the path, we will be all right. But we gotta see if the stove is hot. That's when you get burnt. That's when it's too late, and you need medical attention or someone to put the fire out. My grandmother used to say, "A hard head makes a soft butt."

Anyway, I stayed with both jobs while some billionaire guy bought Morton's and changed everything. Then my two buddies, who I looked up to at Morton's, left for bigger opportunities. So, I began working at Food Lion full-time until they brought in a new general manager, and she was a piece of work. It wouldn't be long before she and I clashed.

3

Jigsaw Puzzle

Ronald

I must give this "Ron-ology" at the beginning of my story for reference: I have discovered that I have become a very complex, unique, charismatic individual. I have several personas inside of my being: Lil Ron, the hurt, abandoned, confused, and angry little boy who lives by the adults' decisions in his life; Ronnie, a wild, rebellious, and self-guided personality who doesn't respect abusive authority, self-righteousness, or disrespect; Ronald, the age-developed adult who is immature, searching for safety, his voice, and the security to be okay with making decisions for Lil Ron, Ronnie, and himself; and Serron, or Sir Ron, the spiritual side of me that was born between 2013 and 2015, as my life transformed and I developed a closer relationship with my Heavenly Father.

My first day of freedom began with a commitment to the effort of change. I didn't know exactly what I would do. Change. How does it happen? What needs to take place? My journey home began on Tuesday, July 10, 2007, from Dillwyn Correctional Center. The moments of that day are very detailed in my memory. As I left the facility that morning, I remember saying to the guard, "Take care. And you will not be seeing me again." Even now, I don't know how much I personally believed that. Always before, I'd leave just to return within a year for some kind of detainment. My hope was different on this day because I wanted to live differently, and dreams had begun to come alive internally that I couldn't express fully at that moment.

A female officer drove me to the Charlottesville bus terminal so I could get a ticket to Richmond. As we made our way to the station, we engaged in a powerful and motivating conversation in which she told me she believed

I could make the change. It was a delicious conversation about my new aspirations and how change is possible if you believe. She asked me about my plans, and I had to inform her that they hadn't really been worked out yet. There were some basic necessities to secure first. I needed to find housing and employment to begin stabilizing my life.

When I arrived at the terminal, something had changed within me. My MO was stolen vehicle, unauthorized use of vehicle, and possession of stolen vehicle, but if I thought like that today, I'd be back on the inside before freedom became a reality. Spiritually, I was in a new place with my creator. I wanted to remain there. My lady got me to the Greyhound station in Charlottesville right on time. I was truly feeling like a new person with a fresh start.

At the terminal, I purchased my ticket, and because prisons give everyone the same clothes to go home in, a formerly incarcerated gentleman recognized me as being newly released. We began a conversation, and I asked to use his phone, which he allowed. I called my mom, Fannie, and when she answered, all my feelings of hurt, despair, and distrust arose in me. Redemption is a road less traveled because it carries memories of moments that are painful and regretful.

* * *

Understand, I wasn't always on the wrong side of the tracks. Things became difficult when I didn't have proper guidance and someone to explain my life as it was happening. Growing up, I began to fight as a way of coping with my challenges. When it became apparent that I had a behavioral health disorder, I was placed in therapy and diagnosed with manic depression. This made me feel crazy, deranged, and quite stupid. I didn't believe any of these things about myself, but therapy was the suggested answer. I became worse. I really began to act out. As a result, Mom Fannie would have to come to the school on a regular basis on account of me being suspended, disrespectful to teachers, or disruptive in class.

I built a space where Mom Fannie no longer trusted my ability to tell her the truth. Before my last incarceration, I caused her to become homeless. According to the lease, I was not supposed to be living with her. And I was using drugs. Management did an emergency entrance into the townhome. They didn't have a search warrant, so no arrests could be made. But she was evicted. Every day of incarceration, I relived the disappointment I had caused her and hoped I could redeem myself someday, in some way.

Eventually, I took an ACEs (Adverse Childhood Experiences) test, a ten-question test about childhood trauma. It asks if you felt unsafe at home, if your parents were drinking, doing drugs, or fighting, and if you were abused verbally, physically, or sexually. Taking this test helped me discover why some of my experiences from childhood to adulthood were showing up in my behaviors and making me feel uncomfortable. Ten is the highest score you can get. I scored eight, which I took to mean I should be medicated or sedated under doctors' orders, because living in society independently wasn't possible. Today, I am beating the odds as well as manifesting a beautiful quality of life.

Fannie is my adoptive mom. I have just begun to speak that truth. I didn't before, out of protectiveness. Many people in her life don't know the whole story of how I came to be her adopted son. She took guardianship when she was forty-three. She adopted me at fifty-five. She is now ninety-three. Explaining it to them after all these years would raise a lot of questions. All this time, they have only known me as her biological son.

She was a good friend of my mother, Deborah K. Savage, and when I was born, Fannie brought me home from the hospital. Fannie, my mom, is a woman of divine spiritual belief. On the day she brought me home, she was forty-three years old, married, with no biological children. However, she has a nurturing spirit and compassionate heart. I would be the first child she raised from birth, and she legally adopted me when I was twelve years old. I changed my name.

Growing up in a strange family dynamic is hard to explain. However, Fannie, my mom, and Debbie, my mother, both played parts in my upbringing. I have two younger sisters and two younger brothers who are considered my blood relatives. I have a host of older siblings who my mom, Fannie, raised or nurtured. With so many different dynamics and spectrums growing up, most of my childhood years, I was deemed a problem. Mom Fannie attempted to give me a normal childhood. However, her education didn't allow for the fundamentals to be there, so I journeyed into discovery and development from many avenues: streets, family, extended family, school, and community.

Mom Fannie, who was the closest person to me, endured all of the anger, pain, harm, resentment, abuse, neglect, and hate that grew inside me as I was practicing being a fun-loving child with a loving heart. Fannie didn't know that I was truly battling with acceptance, and that the more rejection, abandonment, and hurt I experienced, the more I began to withdraw from life. As I entered preteen adolescence, my need to be accepted grew. Drinking and drugs became my outlets. The more withdrawn I became, the more helpless Mom Fannie felt. My rebellious persona, Ronnie, took the stage and began to run and devastate my life.

***

Standing in the Charlottesville bus terminal with a stranger's phone to my ear, I heard Mom's voice, and a peace and calm came over me. But I didn't hear that from her. She was more concerned and worried. She probably felt this way because over many years of traveling down this road of incarceration and release with me, she always hoped each time would be different. This time, I wanted it to be different. I just didn't have the words to express it. I didn't even know what actions I would take to put this change into place. However, I was determined to try. I was excited. I was headed home, where my newfound freedom awaited me.

HOLD UP! I don't have a home. In fact, I am homeless with nowhere to go.

"Mom, can you find a way to the Richmond bus terminal to pick me up?" She'd need to find a ride. I knew it was a lot to ask, but it was all I had.

"I will try," she said. "But I have no money, and you know how people are about their stuff." When the call ended, I felt an emptiness in my soul and was lost in the moment. I wanted this time to be different.

I returned the cell phone to its owner, and we both made our way onto the bus headed to Richmond. Somehow, on a crowded motor coach, we found two seats next to each other. He shared his own story of new beginnings, rejoining society. He told me I might encounter some difficulties on the path to independence and self-sufficiency. All the way there, he was supportive of me finding my hope again. When we arrived in Richmond, I asked him if I could use his phone again. I tried to call Mom, but there was no answer. I thanked him, and he got off the bus. After retrieving my box, I ran inside the terminal in the hopes of asking him one more time, but I could not find him. At that moment, I came to believe in earthly angels. Be careful when entertaining a stranger, because you never know when you are in the company of an angel. That guy was my earthly angel who I never saw again.

My first week home, I was blessed and fortunate to meet friends in recovery who were willing to take a chance on me. I chose to leave Mom's apartment and stay at a recovery house in Richmond. I gained employment at a McDonald's just ten blocks from the recovery house. I really felt blessed and under no stress. This unusual moment was unexplainable. It happened by divine design.

There were rules to living in this recovery house. I had to complete my chores. I had to get groceries. I had to attend twelve-step meetings at least four times a week. I completed these tasks and requirements with ease. However, the house manager, David, didn't approve of how I did my chores. He complained that I didn't do them often enough, and he wasn't satisfied with the way they were completed. I explained to him that I would try my best to improve; however, this situation was new to me. I thanked them for the leg up and continued with the process of recovery.

I was elated that I'd found employment so quickly, and I felt like I should celebrate. However, being an individual in recovery from substance use disorder, I had to find a way to celebrate safely. Modestly, I took my time. I smiled often. I thanked God a lot for the chance to begin this new way of life. I stopped by the probation office to see if I was actually on probation, and was blessed to find out that I was not.

Gratitude was my attitude, and I was so excited that life would be different. I had practiced wrong for so long that wrong seemed right and right felt elusive. Questions shadowed my mind. Past mistakes haunted me. I was scared and frightened, but determination was at my forefront. I was going to try to overcome my past and really see if I could create a life worth living.

There were three of us in the recovery home. I was glad not to be burdening my mom with my worries—I was finally going to be responsible for me. The home's owner, Deneral, who knew me from recovery meetings, trusted my word that I would pay my rent balance once I got my paycheck. I began to build a social network with friends in recovery. Things seemed to be off to a great start. Then trouble began.

One weekend, I decided to travel to Maryland with Marble, my God-sister from recovery meetings, for a recovery cookout. As a result, I was going to be late for the house curfew. I called David, the house manager, and let him speak to Marble. He got the verification he needed; however, he said it wasn't acceptable and told me to be home before curfew. I missed the curfew, and his discipline was two weeks' shut-in, where I would only be allowed to work, go to meetings, and take care of any business. This was not acceptable to me. When I got home, I went to David's room and turned in my key, and he told me to leave.

Being a child who was spoiled and used to seeing things go my way, I had to take responsibility for the situation I'd put myself in. I believed I had made a good choice. But what a mistake I'd made! I'd removed myself from a safe living space and had nowhere to go. Now I had to look for new housing. I packed my stuff and went to live with a coworker from McDonald's. Michael let me move in without knowing each other well, I think, because we were both of the LGBTQIA+ community.

At this time, my life was beginning to take shape. I was dating an older guy named Kerry, and Probation and Parole had released me from the obligation to report. Michael and I worked different shifts, and often I would go out on dates with Kerry. But the freaky side of me had not died yet. One night, I decided to sleep with a young man whom I'd met in jail and who was using drugs. I was not fully aware of the extent of his drug abuse. He told me a sad story and said that he had nowhere to stay. I asked Michael if he could stay with us for a couple of nights, and he said yes.

One night, I worked the night shift with Michael, and he allowed the young man to stay in the house by himself in his room. In the morning, when I got home, Michael told me he was missing about $400. We searched and found the young man, who did not know how much he had taken. But sure enough, he had been using drugs. I felt bad and, wanting to keep the confrontation down, agreed to pay back the money. A moment later, I started thinking about the fact that Michael never could confirm the amount taken. I began to regret my decision. Michael and I got into a confrontation over the dispute, and I no longer felt safe at his house.

When I left Michael's apartment, I had only been home for about six months and again had nowhere to live. Humbly, I asked Kerry if I could stay with him while I continued to recover and pull it back together. He said yes. But we had very different lifestyles and interests. I was issued a contract with the conditions of my stay. One of the rules was no company. After incarceration, that rule seemed like jail all over again. I rebelled and did as I pleased. One day, Kerry, in a moment of rage, cornered me and put his hands on me. I called the police, and he was arrested. As a result, I was put out with no place to go.

I just wanted to live in peace. But making good choices was not my strength.

Ronnie has an uncontrollable rage that, in the past, has led to Ronald making impulsive decisions that have not always landed me in healthy or productive situations. Reflection moment: When I was about seventeen, I got into a relationship with an older man named Charles. We decided to buy a vehicle together. Charles was promiscuous and cheated on me with a boy from the streets, who was our friend. Charles allowed this young man to steal our car, and he could not explain to me why. The car was recovered, but Ronnie wanted revenge. One day after dropping Charles off at work, I stole our car and left the state. I was eventually arrested in South Brunswick, New Jersey, with two friends. After that, Charles and I broke off the relationship.

Another time, when I was still a teenager, I was working for a man named TR. He was married with kids. He was older and would cheat on his wife with many women, and I was attracted to the type of man who was unavailable emotionally, mentally, and physically. Often, I would hope a moment of sexual pleasure would happen between us. On a trip to pick up his daughter in South Carolina, he took me along, as well as a young lady who I knew he was sleeping with. I got angry when TR and the young lady checked into a hotel room. I was asked to stay in the car while they spent intimate time together. Man, I got caught up in the moment. I thought I was special. On our way back to Baltimore with his daughter, TR continued to talk and raised my anger to rage. I asked to be let out of the car when we reached Maryland, where I proceeded to call his wife and let her know of the situation. Ronnie has countless other memories of being vindictive, mean, nasty, and vicious. This carried over into adulthood. It became a trauma that I struggled to heal from.

Coming from inside back to society is hard. Being inside kills that part of you that allows you to be human and humane. My first three years post-release were like undoing a jigsaw puzzle. Living like an animal had become normal. Living life with decent people in regular society was foreign. Love was a blur, and being told what to do was natural. That is partly why many of my early relationships didn't last long.

Today, through my trials, I have learned from my past mistakes and traumas to take more ownership of the person I desire to be and how I want my story to be told. It was apparent that I needed to heal from the sexual traumas and abuse that I suffered from childhood to adulthood if I truly wanted to live a victorious life. I began to seek God on a deeper level so that I could gain knowledge and understanding of the being known as Ronald S. Fountain. My sexual abuse led me to live in fear of love and respect. I was resorting to being needy, always dependent on a mate to give me safety and security. The question I began to ask was: Why was I incapable of giving these things to myself?

***

That question takes me back to October 22, 1996. A time when I truly struggled to love myself. I am sitting in Powhatan Correctional Center, having just received life-changing news. I have been diagnosed with HIV. I believe I will die within two years. I go silent. I don't take medication or adhere to medical advice. Doctors can't explain what exactly is happening in my body. I accept that I will live until death.

Ten years later, after I was released from prison for the last time, I developed shingles. The pain finally forced me to take medication and follow medical care for my diagnosis. Learning to take responsibility for myself and to achieve what was achievable became my mission. For six months, I worked to be responsible in my health care and to love myself better than I had before. Embracing self-love in a stigmatizing society was hard then and is still hard, but it's worth the journey, because I am still here, healthier and stronger than ever before.

4
The Neighborhood

Dave

Spring, 2008. By the time we left my office, it was already dark. It was Ronald's day off from McDonald's, and he'd come to see me and to work on his writing. Afterwards, he asked for a ride home. The recovery house where he was staying was near Mosby Court public housing, just up the hill from the jail where we met. Like most white, middle-class people in Richmond, I knew Mosby Court from driving by it. That night, Ronald took me through it.

Mosby was built in 1962 during the era of urban renewal and massive resistance to school integration. As Ben Campbell explains, "During the period of court-ordered desegregation, a major strategy of Southern resistance was the attempt to promote neighborhood schools as a way of maintaining racial segregation."[6] They built Mosby School to serve Mosby Court public housing. As a result, this part of the city became predominantly poor and Black.

After a series of lefts and rights and lefts, we arrived. Ronald thanked me for the ride and reached for the door. It was then that I realized I did not know how to get home. I did not have a GPS. I did not have a smartphone. I was new to the city, and most days I walked. I leaned toward the windshield, searching the dark for a street sign or landmark. Ronald chuckled, touched my arm, and pointed.

"Dave, that's 23rd! Hit that and take a right. Five blocks down is your street."

How had I missed it? I pass 23rd all the time when I walk to campus. Was it because I had never been this far north on 23rd? Was it because I was here at night? Was it because I was in a car at night in the projects with someone I had met in jail? It was all of those things. It was none of those things. I had not imagined Ronald getting out of jail and living in this neighborhood. I had never imagined him as a neighbor.

Technically, he was not in the same neighborhood as me. I was in Church Hill—specifically, a smaller, gentrified part of the much bigger, older, historically Black neighborhood—and he was in Union Hill, right next door. But a neighborhood is not just geographical. It is social, communal. The best neighborhoods are formed and informed by people sharing their time and space. It is not about where the borders are drawn but how people come together.

There are no discernible borders in *Mister Rogers' Neighborhood*. Each episode of the children's show starts with a bird's-eye view of the streets, then quickly gives way to a swell of vibraphone, a glissando on the piano, and Mister Rogers singing the question that you already know how to answer. Of course, you will be his neighbor!

Mister Rogers is always welcoming someone into his home. Someone he knows or someone he is meeting for the first time. They offer what they have, what they know. It is less important *what* they share than *that* they share. This is the essence of the neighborhood, this welcoming and sharing, not the policing of borders, of who belongs and who does not.

A few years after Fred Rogers started his show, an integrated group of protestors jumped into the swimming pool at the Monson Motor Lodge in St. Augustine, Florida. They were protesting the white owner's refusal to let Martin Luther King Jr. and his guests eat at the motel restaurant. Seeing the integrated group of people in his pool, the owner dumped acid into the water. Someone captured it on film, and that clip was seen around the country.[7] Against a backdrop of TV news like this, Mister Rogers offered an alternative. In a now-famous episode of his show, Officer Clemmons, who is Black, comes to visit Mister Rogers on a hot day. Rogers invites him to cool off in his wading pool.

"It does look enjoyable," Officer Clemmons says. "But I don't have a towel or anything."

Mister Rogers smiles. "Oh, you share mine." The men take off their shoes. The camera lingers on their feet, side by side, Black and white.[8] The vibraphone mingles with the lapping water as the camera slow-zooms in on their feet. It is so ordinary but, for the time, so political.

Ronald did not just show me how to get home that night. He showed me where I was—and who I was—in the neighborhood. He needed a ride. I needed directions. We shared what we had. That was a beautiful day in the neighborhood.

5
The Job

Dave

Fall, 2008. "The turn's coming up, Dave!" I would have missed it. Kelvin was all fired up. I was still trying to wake up. It was 8 a.m. on a Saturday. I am not usually out of the house that early. I was also distracted. A woman in a long, flowing, aqua dress was speed walking by us in white heels. It made no sense. Nothing was open. Nothing was stirring on the Southside of Richmond. Just a play of morning light on the warehouses.

We were looking for the Sliver and Splinter carpentry shop. The owner, Alton, is a friend from church. He always asks me about the guys from the class at the jail. Last Sunday, I told him that Kelvin was out and had a job, but he needed a second job to make more money so that he could buy a car. Alton thought he might be able to help. He asked me to bring Kelvin over for an interview.

"You're going to like Alton," I said as we drove. "Easy to talk to. Got that strong Kentucky accent."

"I already know I'm going to like him, Dave. He's friends with you."

I took a right, slowed down, and parallel parked. We gathered our things, opened the doors, stepped to the curb, and there she was. Barely there in that aqua dress, all bones and almond skin. Her eyes, sleepless, were locked on Kelvin's.

"I need you," she said in a choked whisper. Kelvin hunched his shoulders, minimizing their height difference. A deep concern bloomed over his face.

"You don't need me," he said quietly. He tried moving toward the door of the shop. She blocked him. He sighed, shook his head, and stepped back.

If she noticed me at all, she did not let on. I felt like an extra on a movie set standing just outside the frame. I was there but not in the shot.

"Look, I'm just out here to handle some business," Kelvin said. The woman tugged a gold necklace slung low on her chest and pursed her lips. He shook his head. She caught a shiver. He grunted. Her face spasmed. He shook his head again. Her arms stiffened. For a second, I thought she was going to slug him. Then they just stared at each other like gunslingers at high noon until she suddenly spun hard to the left and took off the same way she'd come. After she clicked around the corner, Kelvin let out the breath I did not realize he was holding.

"I always hated selling to people like that," he reflected. What? I thought she was selling to him. I thought she was a prostitute. Why else would she be dressed for the evening so early in the morning?

"Oh! Okay. I understand." I really didn't. He obviously didn't know her. Why would she think he was selling? I decided to just go with it. "Why did that bother you?"

Kelvin looked at me like I might never understand anything.

"Because, Dave! I always thought maybe I'd be the *last* one that sells to someone like her."

He reached for the door.

Light filled the stairwell. The smell of cut lumber and glue filled my nose. Alton greeted us at the top of the stairs in a muted flannel shirt with a carpenter's pencil and a small pad of paper in the front pocket. His hair was wavy, brown, and salted. His beard was thick, grey, and trimmed, suggesting both vitality and age.

"Did you find the place okay?" We nodded. He led us to high stools near the table saws and lathes. He pointed out the different projects, explaining his work. Periodically, he'd pause to make a quick drawing or to tell a story. His parents had fostered more than fifty children in Kentucky. He still saw many of them at family reunions. Some had problems with the law, he added, but they got through it. Kelvin reciprocated, sharing what he knew about carpentry, his experiences growing up in Richmond, including what he called his "knucklehead days" of selling drugs. Alton folded his hands in his lap and tilted his head to one side.

"What is it that you really want in life, Kelvin? Not just from this job, but long-term?"

"To be truthful? I want to coach basketball. I want to help kids who need that guidance and support that I needed coming up. I want to help them get to college, get a scholarship, maybe even make the NBA." Alton hired him on the spot.

Months later, I thought about the three of us on those high stools as I flew to Memphis for the annual meeting of the Rhetoric Society of America. I was going to be on a panel with other professors who had also taught writing classes in prison. We were going to get into the promise of it, the ethics of it, the joy of it. But as I read over my paper, I began wondering more about the outcomes we cannot foresee in jail and cannot prepare for—the connections between writing and change that only emerge after jail, when you drive one of your former students to a job interview.

The conference was at the Peabody Hotel in Memphis, one of those old-school places rich with Southern charm. A white marble fountain fills the lobby. Gold sconces line the walls. Polished wood rafters frame the ceiling. And, I was told, there were ducks. The tradition formed during the Great Depression. A few hunters, drinking whiskey, let some of their live decoy ducks out of their bags and into the fountain for a laugh. No one complained, and eventually people realized there was money to be made. People would pay to see the ducks walk a red carpet in the lobby. The hotel started charging. They even built a royal duck palace on the roof of the hotel for the ducks to live in—a $200,000 structure made of marble, glass, and bronze. [9]

After I checked in, I left to see the Lorraine Motel, the place where Martin Luther King Jr. was assassinated in 1968, now a Civil Rights museum. On my walk to the Lorraine, I saw a half dozen young Black men in matching T-shirts crouching on their hands and knees on a strip of green plastic with their heads down. They formed a long wall. A crowd had gathered. The street was closed to traffic. A beat dropped. Then a man sprinted toward those turtled backs, sprang high, tucked, flipped, and sailed over the line of men, landing hard, perfect, on both feet. For the next twenty minutes, the others took turns defying gravity until, at last, they passed the bucket, and my heart rate dropped back to normal.

King was not supposed to be in Memphis the day he got shot. He'd added Memphis to his itinerary because the city's sanitation workers were striking to demand safer working conditions and better pay, and King wanted to join them. He had been scheduled to stay at the Peabody. But at the last minute, he switched his reservation to the Lorraine, a Black-owned business that he wanted to support.[10]

There is not much to the Lorraine. Light blue doors. White vertical blinds. Two stories facing a parking lot. They have the museum set up so you can see King's room from behind a velvet rope. They took out the wall, so that it seems like you are in the room. On a table by the bed are his Bible, his reading glasses, and a heavy black phone. In the corner, an open suitcase. Over there, on the table, a cup of coffee. A pack of cigarettes. The room was ripe with humanity. I left pained in a way that I could not name.

When I got back to the Peabody, the ducks were making their way to the fountain. Cameras and kids were held aloft. The mood was festive, the crowd large and dressy as an Episcopal Church picnic. It pissed me off. Ducks that cannot fly were likely earning more money for their handlers than Black men flying over the asphalt. More than striking sanitation workers. More than Kelvin working two jobs so that he could buy a car and drive kids to basketball practice.

In 1967, the year before he was assassinated, King delivered a speech in Chicago that made an uncompromising critique of capitalism. He said, "We must devote at least as much to our children's education and the health of the poor as we do to the care of our automobiles and the building of beautiful, impressive hotels. We must also realize that the problems of racial injustice and economic injustice cannot be solved without a radical redistribution of political and economic power."[11]

When King died, the people in Memphis protested. Downtown was boarded up. The National Guard was called in. A tank that looked straight out of World War II rolled into town and patrolled near the Peabody.[12] Memphis looked like a European city recently liberated from fascism.

Five years later, in 1973, the Peabody closed. The owners were in debt.[13] It would take many years and millions of dollars before it could reopen. The Lorraine became a national Civil Rights museum in 1991.[14] But to many, it served less as a unifying force than as a reminder of old wounds that had never properly healed over in the fight for jobs.[15]

6
Ministry

Dave

Spring, 2009. The wood table was polished to a high gloss. The edge was beveled and inlaid with gold. Bookshelves ran from the ceiling to the floor. Wingback chairs looked out from the corner. There was a dictionary on a wooden stand. A globe by the fireplace. A small card catalog. It was an unlikely place for a meeting about prisoner reentry. But when Terence got home from prison and shared with me his vision of a ministry for people getting out of prison, I wanted to help him.

We met in the library at St. Paul's Episcopal Church, near Shockoe Bottom, across the street from the Capitol. St. Paul's was once known as the Cathedral of the Confederacy. Jefferson Davis was a member. Many of the other members of the church owned slaves. But history is only as strong as the people telling it. By the time I began attending in 2005, St. Paul's had become known for its outreach ministries, some of which had come to include prison. Those ministries had gone dormant, so I had been told. I sensed an opportunity to awaken them.

We sat at a round table in the library with Wallace Adams-Riley, the rector of the church, and Pastor Benjamin Harris, an ex-offender, pastor of St. Stephen's Koinonia Church in Church Hill, and an entrepreneur who had a ministry for people getting out of prison: training them to sell dress shirts and ties door-to-door. One of my students from the jail, G, was in that ministry. Dean was in Harris's mentorship program.

Terence was passionate about the foundation, as he described it. It would be different from the other nonprofit services that treated you like a client in some overworked person's caseload. This would be more like a brotherhood of people who had done time and knew how to make a way out of no way. It was a heartfelt if somewhat paradoxical vision. He needed the kind of help he wanted to give. It was also, at times, a hard vision to understand. I could not tell how many people would be working with him, who would do what, how many people they would serve, or where the work would take place. But I told myself that this was why we were having the meeting, to lay it all on that polished round table.

After Terence finished sharing his vision, he sat back and planted his elbows on his thighs, listening without looking at Pastor Harris, who was now telling us a story of someone he'd tried to help who got out of prison. Harris got him a job. He got him to go to church. Things were going well. Then the man disappeared. He couldn't find him anywhere. He couldn't get him on the phone. Months later, when he saw him on the street, he said the man smelled rank and looked anxious. Harris confronted him. The man admitted he was using crack. He was also selling it. In fact, he needed to sell this bag tonight so that he could get paid. Harris asked him what he would do with the money, and the man confessed he was going to buy more crack, but for himself this time. Selling was the only way he could keep using. Terence lifted his chin and looked at Harris.

"What did you do?" he asked him.

"We have to be willing to do the hard thing," Harris said to the room as he formed a steeple with his hands and leaned across the table. We grew quiet, wondering about that hard thing.

"I told him . . . sell it to me." I flinched.

"We have to be willing to do the hard thing," Harris said again, creasing his forehead in resolve. He went on to explain: First, he got the man some food. Then, he got him a motel room. When they were safe inside, he bought the crack and walked it into the bathroom. The man followed him. Harris dropped the little baggie into the toilet and gestured toward the handle. With tears in his eyes, the man pushed the handle. They prayed together as the currents pulled the drugs away.

"Amen!" Terence said. "That's the kind of involvement I'm seeking, too. Yes. To meet people in those moments of need." They regarded each other with solemn nods.

The meeting broke up with assurances of a job well done and promises to meet again. Then I drove Terence home. He was living with his mother, not too far from St. Paul's. That was temporary, though, he assured me. Soon he'd be on his own. Soon, he would start the foundation. He grew animated as his future fell into place. He would be doing God's work and getting paid! I parked the car. He invited me in, shouting ahead to his mother that he'd brought the professor with him.

"Wait here," he said, leaving me in a living room filled with muted colors and soft furniture. It was the room of someone who took the time to control the smallest of details—this coaster here, that lamp there—so that the whole room was neat and orderly from any angle. His mother was no less commanding. Regal, beautiful, she greeted me not so much as a friend of her son but as *the professor* who had come calling unannounced. She invited me to sit . . . there. Then she sat across from me and regarded me for a moment before speaking.

"So, you're the professor who started the writing class at the jail," she finally said. I told her all about the class. As I spoke, I remembered what Terence had written about his childhood with her in Gilpin Court public housing. I had never imagined meeting the woman he had written about, the one who was constantly working and too tired to explain to him where his father was or why he couldn't do this, go there, have that. She was never too tired to beat him, though. Terence returned from the kitchen with two big cans of Natural Ice beer. He smiled as he showed them to me. I was not planning on staying long, so I shook my head and gestured for him to go ahead.

"Get him a Pepsi then!" his mother ordered. He turned toward the kitchen, muttering as he went. We listened to the fridge door opening and closing, then the slow tread of Terence returning to the living room, Pepsi in hand.

"And a glass with ice!" she chided, shaking her head at me. I sighed helplessly with her as I watched the man become a boy again, who could still not do anything right in his mother's home. Terence shuffled away and returned with a glass filled with ice. I set the glass down on the coaster and cracked the can. A slow hiss filled the space between us.

I started to talk about writing as a way of figuring out your life. She listened patiently, then interrupted.

"Shouldn't a man at this age have figured that out by now?" There was no easy way of answering. This was her son. He was sitting right there. If I conceded her point that, come middle age, a man should know what to do with his life, I would be minimizing the feelings he had poured into his story, which connected his lost feeling in life back to his childhood. If I took his side, I would be on that razor edge of blaming her or her situation for how he fared in life.

"It takes some people longer than others," I suggested. She pursed her lips and grunted. She thanked me for helping Terence. I thanked her for the Pepsi. Then I announced that I had to get home. Terence picked up his beer, put the other unopened can in his pocket, and walked me to the car. He thanked me for the ride and for the meeting at the church. I pulled away from the curb and into the dark, empty street. I saw him in my rearview, walking away, drinking, thinking.

The next week, Terence showed up at my office unannounced. He was flustered, talking quickly and loudly. It was in between classes. There was a crush of people right outside my open office door.

"Slow down! Start from the beginning. And sit down!"

"Dave, I'm trying to tell you! And no, I won't sit down! Now, I'm gonna tell you again so you can really hear it." He stood as close to me as possible and slowed the story way down, raising his voice and over-enunciating like some people do for little kids or old people. "I—was—walking. Okay? Walking! In—the—neighborhood! A big group formed. Beyond them was the police."

"The police? What were they doing there?"

"That's what I asked! But the people didn't know. They told me they were afraid to pass through because they didn't want to get searched. This one old guy in particular. He had a little bit of weed on him, and he was freaking out! I mean, Dave! It was half a joint! A roach, really. Not enough to do anything."

"Were you drinking?"

"What? What does that have to do with anything? I had a beer!" Then he thought more about it and lowered his voice a bit. "Two beers. And I brought one of those hard lemonades with me. It wasn't open."

"Okay, so what did you do?"

"I told the old man with the joint, Give it to me. I'll carry it for you. You can follow me." But when they reached the barricade, the police told them no, turn around. This was a crime scene. Somehow, Terence resisted—physically, verbally, I could not tell. The police grabbed him, shoved him against their car, handcuffed him, and hurt him. He showed me the marks.

The hard lemonade broke open in his pocket. They searched his other pocket and found the roach. He was arrested for trespassing and taken to the magistrate at the city jail, where they charged him with trespassing and resisting arrest. He avoided jail but was ordered to take an anger management class. Now, in the office, he was at the apex of his anger as he finished the story, drawing the glances of the students in the hall.

"I was out there in ministry, and this is what they do!"

I stepped fast to shut the door. It took some willpower not to slam it. I felt my heart up high in my chest.

"You are going to sit down now, shut up, and listen to me," I said. He dropped into the seat with a quiet "yes, sir." I had never spoken to him like that. I had never felt the need. His face was a blend of teenage insolence and mature concern that I was about to lose it. I *was* about to lose it.

"To you, it was ministry. To the police, it was someone with beer on his breath and more alcohol and weed on him."

"It was a lemonade!" he protested.

"I'm not going to argue about the lemonade."

He slumped back in his chair, grumbling and shaking his head, retreating into his own foregone conclusions about how I had misread the story.

"I'm not taking sides, Terence. What they did was atrocious. But I don't care about them. I care about you. There are other ways to do ministry. Better ways. You need to find them." I took a deep breath and sat down.

"Can I speak now?"

"Yes, I'm done."

"It's easy for you to say Don't go there. Don't do that. You're not in ministry."

"I'm not?"

"You have to go where the people are."

"How did I meet you?"

"Oh, my God! I know *that*! We're not talking about *that*!" We were talking about ministry—how, where, and why to do it.

Father Gregory Boyle, the founder and director of Homeboy Industries in Los Angeles, the largest gang intervention program in the world, describes ministry as an act of widening the circle of our humanity in such a way that no one is left outside. He writes, "The measure of our compassion lies not in our service of those on the margins but in our willingness to see ourselves in kinship with them." Kinship enables us to break down the boundaries of "us" and "them."[16] It enables you to do things you did not think you could do. Buying someone's crack. Holding someone's roach. Listening to someone's vision of a ministry for people getting out of prison.

7

People, Places, and Things

Dave

Fall, 2009. Something had come over Ronald. A few minutes ago, he was spinning freely into Bible quotes and aphorisms. His voice was elevated. His mood was ebullient. He seemed taller than his five feet standing up there in front of the students in my prison literature class at VCU. But now, sitting by my office window in the late-day light, he looked small as a child. His eyes were closed. He breathed slowly through his nose. Terence and I sat watching him, talking to each other discreetly with our eyes. Across the hall, someone was lecturing in a low monotone broken up now and again with a guttural cough. At last, Ronald opened his eyes.

"I have an announcement," he said. "I've given this a lot of thought. So, I hope you'll be able to support me." He took a big belly breath, let it out, and looked at me. Then he looked at Terence. "Okay. I'm just going to say it. I quit my job at McDonald's."

"Woah!" Terence jerked back like he'd just missed a foul ball to the head. "Woah!" he shouted again, louder, like we were actually at a ballpark. "This is reentry! This is what it means! Black men with records can't be *quitting* jobs! You just got promoted to manager!"

Ronald turned to me to defend himself from Terence.

"They was going to put me at a store all the way out on the West End, Dave. I can't get there without a car. It would take forever on the bus."

"So, you take the bus!" Terence countered. Ronald implored me to say something.

"Why not just stay at the store on Broad? It's on the bus line," I offered. He shook his head.

"Someone was stealing from the till. They was getting high out back but trying to pin it on me. I can't be around that." I opened my mouth and heard Terence.

"That's everywhere! You can't run from that!"

He had a good point. They say to stay clean, you need to change people, places, and things. But is that true, or even possible? The Big Book of Alcoholics Anonymous says, "People have said we must not go where liquor is served." They say the "only chance for sobriety would be someplace like the Greenland Ice Cap, and even there an Eskimo might turn up with a bottle of scotch and ruin everything." The solution is not to rid the world of alcohol but to rid yourself of your "alcoholic mind."[17] Or your cocaine mind, or heroin mind, or whatever is your drug of choice. Moving away from the people, places, and things that trigger you can help, but it is not the root of the solution.

"You didn't let me finish, Terence. I only told you the first half." Ronald paused like someone about to rip off a Band-Aid. "I'm moving back to Baltimore."

Terence exploded in disbelief. "And what do you think you'll find there?"

"Chance and opportunity," Ronald barely said. He looked like he might cry.

"Ain't no different there than what you got here!" A few students in the front row of the class across the hall looked up, alarmed. The legato notes of the lecture were no match for the staccato in Terence's voice.

"Hey," I stage-whispered. "There's a class going on out there." I got up to close the door. When I sat down again, Terence gave me the side-eye. How could I be so petty? A man's life is on the line here, and you're worried about people out there?

Ronald went on to explain that Richmond was where he got incarcerated. He associated it with that time in his life. And Richmond was not really home. Baltimore was home. A bigger city, too. He would find more people living alternative lifestyles, more job opportunities, and more places to go where he did not need a car.

The interrogation ended an hour later. It took some time before the three of us could wrap up and walk out into the hallway, down the stairs, and into the sunlight.

"This is not goodbye," Ronald said. "I'll be back."

I was happy that he was going but could not wrest myself from the worry. He was homeless now. He was jobless. What would he do? Somehow, he knew my thoughts.

"You know I'm on a spiritual journey now, right? This is all going according to God's plan." His smile was buoyant and big again, like it had been in class.

"I'll be okay, Dave. I'll call you when I get there."

I nodded. Terence nodded. Then we parted, each man heading away to his own place.

8

Transformative Justice

Ronald

My discontent led to my irresponsibility that led to me being fired from McDonald's. Blind faith begins to show up: *I am content with moving back to Baltimore.* I am speaking what I want to be true, despite what is happening in my reality. *I believe my journey in Baltimore will be better than my journey in Richmond.*

I was selfish in my decision to go, considering that my mom didn't want me to leave her, and my twelve-step fellowship was divided about whether I could make it. I tell you today, when I think back on it, I admit it sounds crazy.

Before leaving, I met with Robert, my sponsor from recovery meetings, who was showing me how to live this new way of life. When we met, we decided to pray and have a truth moment. Then Robert made two statements that encouraged me to move to Baltimore. He said, "God has you," and "You are not the same person you were before." In April 2009, my decision was etched in stone when I attended the Chesapeake & Potomac Regional Recovery Convention in Ocean City, Maryland. After that, I made the journey back to the city where I was born.

My presence back in Baltimore was welcomed by evil. I started going to the club and ran into my next relationship, Anthony. From his appearance, he was a man of stature. I spent a whole weekend with him, and it was like a dream come true. I moved in, and what began as lust became love, with me believing this was my knight in shining armor. Our first six months were a honeymoon period of endless good moments. Then I began to make Anthony feel unappreciated. He began to deny me sexual fulfillment, and I resorted to cheating. Anthony was cheating as well; however, he set a trap that I fell right into with an associate of his. When that happened, his mood changed drastically. He became hard and condescending to me.

I was taught by Mom Fannie and Mother Debbie to never let anyone who says they love me beat or mistreat me. One day, during a heated discussion, Anthony hit me, and I was afraid to tell anyone. We had friendship counseling. Anthony confessed that he'd hit me in a moment of rage. I confirmed this, and we thought we could heal from it. But the outcome was uncertain.

* * *

I am a big flirt. Generally, all it takes is a hi.

I get off the bus on the night of June 22, 2009, at about 11:30 p.m., during the last moments of my birthday. As I walk the pavement path to the house I share with my brother's family, I see this handsome young guy coming down the street toward me. He's dark and a little taller than me. The closer we get to each other, the sexier he gets. As we pass each other, I speak.

"Hi, how are you doing?"

"Fine, just broke. I can't get home." He walks toward some townhomes and motions to a guy on the left. That gesture gets my attention. I don't know how to take that. I walk past the first guy and am relieved to leave them both behind me. Almost home. I smile and thank God for my safety. Then I look down at the ground and see a shadow that's not mine. I turn around. It's the second guy. My heart stops when I see the gun. *Why?* All the years I spent in the streets getting high, no gun has ever been pulled on me. My sensor must be off.

"I have no money," I tell him in a panicked voice.

"Don't make me shoot you."

I pull away in the wrong direction. He grabs the strap of my backpack. My backpack breaks free. I scream and yell for help while holding on to my backpack. It must have scared him, because he let go and ran. I turn and run, too.

Once inside my house, I look out the window and, Lord, have mercy! I see the townhouse that the two guys go into! Wow, what should I do? My brother has already left for work. I don't want to cause a panic with my brother's girl and my nieces in the house.

I call my newest friend, Maurice, who I met at the McDonald's in Baltimore, where I work. Maurice is a slender, older, nicely aged man who finds me delightful. I know he's attracted to me. When Maurice answers, I quickly tell him what happened. The beast in Maurice shows up, and all of a sudden, this mild man sounds like an army of ten. What I didn't know is that his nephews came from gangster ways.

I finally remember to pray. It's what I should have been doing at first, and so, yes, I pray aloud into the phone. Maurice doesn't even hear me. He just wants to come and bring noise to the apartment down the street. Noise is street talk for causing damage, hurt, and wickedness to a threat. I am trying to calm Maurice down, telling him to PAUSE—pray and use spiritual energy. But he is already readying for war.

"What's your address?" he demands.

"Good, you don't know where I'm at!"

"I know the area, and I will show up and find you!"

I am gripped by fear. My brother is not home, but his family is. I don't want to cause alarm. But I had to tell someone. Now, the way Maurice is talking makes me think we could all go to jail.

I give him my address and tell him to come alone, please. I tell him I need to talk with him first. He tries to get me to allow him to bring his cousins. We agree to meet and speak first and go from there.

Maurice makes his way to me, and I tell him the whole situation. I let him know that I don't want to bring any danger to my brother's house because my nieces are there as well. I know I have only one chance to get this right, so we decide to ride around to see if we see the guys again. I recognize one of the guys, and he runs into the townhome and hides. I am now sure I know which door he ran into. Maurice's blood begins to boil. He is on a rampage again and wants street justice. I calm him down again and reaffirm that I want to go about this the right way. I eventually get through to Maurice, and he drops me off. I let him know I will keep him posted with the details when I call the police. He is delighted with that and goes home.

I call the police and inform them that I have been mugged at gunpoint. They come pretty quickly to take my report. I give them all the details, and they ask if I'm sure I can point out the exact house. I say yes, and they proceed to the door. Their knocks get no answer, so they go to the courthouse to get a search warrant to enter the premises, while I stay behind in a police car. I am nervous because I have never done this before, and I don't want to send my brothers to jail. It is the first time in a very long time that I've been on this side of the law.

While I wait, I call my former boyfriend, Anthony, for moral support. He answers, and I begin to explain what happened. He gives me a listening ear and tries to be empathetic. He's an hour away in DC, but I want him to drop all responsibility and come to Baltimore. Then the police return with the warrant, and I need to get off the phone. I tell Anthony I will call him as soon as I can and let him know how I'm doing.

The police ask me again if I am sure of the townhome. I assure them, yes, and they proceed to surround the house. As I hear them banging on the door, my heart begins to beat very fast. I am nervous and anxious, as if I was the one who committed a crime. The men do not answer the door. The townhome is dark. The police shout a warning that they're coming in, and then they kick in the door. The search for the suspects begins. They find them hiding in the upstairs rooms as if they have been asleep the whole time. They recover the men, as well as the gun. A young lady is also arrested for obstruction of justice. The police tell me they need nothing else from me until I come to court.

In the following weeks, my life returns to normal, somewhat. I am nervous and torn about what to say in court. I go back and forth in my mind. I don't like using the police to handle my business. I know what jail is like and don't want to send my fellow brothers to jail like I had been sent so many times before. But I also know that what those guys did is bad.

When I receive the court notice, I contemplate not showing up. Prayer and meditation are on my side. The Lord is my strength. I show up for the court date as scheduled. The prosecuting attorney comes into the room where I am waiting. My nerves are on edge. My heart is racing. The attorney informs me that I won't need to testify. The men are pleading guilty to the charges. They have other cases in Baltimore County. I breathe a sigh of relief. I leave the courtroom that day, realizing I am living on the right side of the law. But I also understand that there will be some difficult decisions ahead of me.

* * *

August 20, 2010. After a late shift at McDonald's, I call Anthony and ask him to pick me up. He's living with me in Baltimore now, but he refuses. So, I take the bus. I get off at my stop and start to walk the few blocks home when I am approached by a young man asking for change. I give him the little that I have. Two blocks from my house, he shows up again and pushes me up against a fence by the railroad track. At first, I think he's trying to do something sexual. Then a buddy of his walks up and talks to him. I pull away and escape down the hill. When I reach the street, I run. However, I am not gaining enough speed. I run to the first house and collapse on the lawn. They catch up to me. One of them punches me in the face, and I faint. When I come to, I realize they have stolen my belongings. Something is telling me to get up. I make my way up the street, where I discover that I am bleeding from my side. I pray to God and believe this is not my end.

I see a lady with a man, and I try to ask her for help. She has a scared look in her eyes and moves away from me. I keep making my way home. When I get there, I knock on the door and lie down on the porch. Anthony comes to the door. All I can say is *call an ambulance*. He does, and when the paramedics arrive, they attempt to pick me up. I tell them I have been stabbed on my right side. When my lover hears that, he runs out of the house and down the street. He comes back as they are putting me in the ambulance. I faint again. The bumps in the road bring me back to consciousness. I feel great pain in my side. I am thirsty.

When we arrive at Johns Hopkins Hospital, I am rushed to the back, where they immediately take X-rays. The doctor comes to tell me that I have a collapsed lung and need emergency surgery. I'm told I can't be put to sleep for the surgery. However, they will numb the area to alleviate the pain. I cannot refuse, even though I want to out of fear. I agree, and I am prepared for surgery. It goes fine. No complications. I am admitted to the hospital for recovery.

I am a person in long-term recovery from substance use disorder. But I have to be put on narcotics—a push-button painkiller. Whenever I press the button, it instantly relieves the pain. Without thought, for the first twenty-four hours, I enjoy the high. Every time I come to, I press the button. After a day of this, the nurses informed me that they needed to put me on pills because I wouldn't stay conscious long enough for them to talk to me. I start the pills, and the fog from the high begins to wear off.

When I was in the emergency room, I asked to see Anthony. However, because I hadn't talked with the police yet, he was denied entry. That first night was a blur. I remember speaking to the detectives assigned to my case. They were men of African descent, very detail-oriented and handsome. They took all my information and said they would contact me when I left the hospital. My sponsor from recovery meetings came to see me as soon as I informed him where I was. I didn't want many people to know where I was, so I didn't have many visitors.

After three days in the hospital, the doctors told me I'm doing good and can finish recovering at home. The incident happened on a Friday, and I was released from the hospital on Sunday with the staples still in place, shocked by the blessing of God's healing. I am given a prescription for Percocet, which I give to my lover to hold for me so that I won't abuse them. I can bear the pain. I only take one to sleep the first night. After that, my lover tells me he threw them away.

This journey with justice is different from the first time I was robbed. This suspect is hard to find. His movement is at night, and the detectives work during the day. We spent two months trying to put a case together. The efforts fail. The suspects are never found. I stop contacting the detectives and focus more on my healing and recovery from the traumatic experience.

After my two encounters with perpetrators, my view of the criminal justice system really takes on new meaning. I incorporate it into my calling. I created an organization called LIVE: Lifting Individual Voices for Empowerment. The goal is to help formerly incarcerated people, LGBTQIA+ people, and elders set relevant life-planning goals and find resources, while supporting their efforts to remove barriers so they can see themselves and be successful. Through this work, I am correcting the lens through which I've viewed myself, my family, my friends, and the world. I am growing to know more of myself. My life taught me to fight. With LIVE, I begin to sell a new kind of justice system that would transform instead of reform. I am pursuing a complete change of the system, not just tinkering with parts of it while letting it work in essentially the same way.

I am on a personal crusade for transformative justice, not just in the criminal justice system but in all aligning systems, like politics and social services. I want to help society stop creating criminals. We could learn through the experiences of our communities if we took the time to listen. Life could be fair if we took the time to search for the truth about why people suffer and how they can heal.

9
Redemption

Dave

Summer, 2009. We were halfway over the Manchester Bridge when Andre told me to slow down. I tapped the brakes. The sky was starless. The road was pebbly. He leaned toward me to look out of my window. His trim mustache and beard framed his lips in a circle.

"Right there." He pointed to a cement post jutting out from the corner close to the road. "That's where we crashed." It had been another night on the Manchester Bridge. Another night in a stack of nights that he was trying to fill without heroin, the last time he got out of prison. That night, he had visited his old neighborhood, Jackson Ward, just to be around the kind of people he knew from the streets. But he soon tired of that since most of the ones he really knew and loved were dead. He decided to go home, but didn't have a ride. A car came by carrying three people he kind of knew. They offered him a ride.

Within a few minutes, he found himself in the middle of a high-speed police chase. The guy next to him threw a gun out the window. The driver sped up, broke through a police barrier, and crashed in the spot that Andre had just shown me. The people fled. Andre stayed. When the police came out, guns drawn and shouting, he got out of the car, put his hands up, stated his name, and said he was just a passenger and didn't know anything. The police beat him, cuffed him, brought him to the station, and beat him again. He passed out. They did an illegal cavity search. He woke up in jail, completely nude and cold. Unbeknownst to him, the car he was in had been involved in dozens of robberies. Without any other suspects, the police pinned all the charges on Andre.

He had been out of prison for a few months that night I drove him home. Later that year, in December, toward the end of the semester, he read the story of that police chase in draft form to VCU students in my prison literature class. His delivery was almost stoic, which drew even more attention to the police brutality. He was just relating what happened, not pleading for sympathy. And this was not even the ending of the story. He'd had a jury trial, which he explained was unusual. Most guys take a plea. Also unusual: He represented himself. Very few people do that. And he beat every charge.

As he told the story, he did not brag, not even a little. He spoke with the humility of a pitcher at a press conference, explaining his no-hitter game by generalizing the principles of good pitching. He relaxed into his theme of overcoming the odds when he stopped reading and added that he had a job now and had just passed the test to become a fireman, which had been his childhood dream.

That dream was derailed when his father got him hooked on heroin in middle school.

When he was in prison drafting that story in letters, I wrote back asking where his father was now and what he was doing. "The sanity of my father is unknown," he said. "He looks like a Black bin Laden, the hair and the beard." It was not an image I could relinquish. Was that his father by the homeless shelter across from the police station? He was not tall like Osama bin Laden, but he had a grey-black beard running down a long face. I did not approach him the first time that I saw him. I built my case slowly over a month of passing him on my walks to campus.

He was squatting on the sidewalk curb by the corner of the building. He held a big Styrofoam cup of coffee in both hands like a prayer. His clothes hung loosely from his rail-thin body. His eyes were rummy.

"Hi!" I said in a too-cheery voice. I sounded like some do-gooder from a church. A social worker in training. I didn't recognize myself. "How are you doing today?"

"Fiiiine," he replied, stretching the word into a whine like a kid forced to use his manners.

"Are you Gregory Simpson?" Ever so slowly, he shook his head, coffee misting between us. He did not ask why I had asked. He did not say anything else. He just turned away, rendering me invisible. And I wondered: What would I have said if he had answered yes? Why was I sleuthing in another man's life?

MAN KILLED IN POLICE CHASE WAS A LONGTIME FELON – AND GUEST LECTURER AT VCU[18]

The news made the front page of the *Richmond Times-Dispatch*. December 8, 2009. Three days after he visited my class to tell the story of surviving that police chase over the Manchester Bridge, defending himself in the trial, and landing a job with the city, Andre robbed a gas station near my house and fled the scene with his driver. Both men died in the car chase. In the news story, I was named as the professor who had invited him to campus to "lecture" and who was also helping him get published.

There was a comments section in the online version of the article. Most were critical of the police for watching the robbery from the parking lot of the convenience store and then initiating a high-speed chase that ran Andre and his driver off the road. They were sad for the men who lost their lives, as well as for their loved ones who grieved for them. Some found it admirable that I had tried to help Andre through the writing class. Others called me an idiot for believing prisoners could change. One called me a typical liberal who thought there was "art in the gutter."

Another commentator likened me to Norman Mailer, the novelist who corresponded with Jack Henry Abbott in the 1970s. Abbott was a state-raised convict in a maximum-security prison who had endured all forms of torture, including solitary confinement, food and light deprivation, psychotropic drugs, and random beatings. In prison, he killed a man who threatened him. When he was paroled to New York City—in large part because of the support he had from Mailer—he killed a waiter in a café, then fled. While he was in hiding, his book, *In the Belly of the Beast*, published with Mailer's help, was climbing *The New York Times* bestseller list.

I had a hard time seeing myself like Mailer. He bonded with Abbott in a manly way about the code of violence amongst prisoners and the violence between prisoners and guards. Abbott's writing is brutal. There are no temperate moments. No vulnerability. This, of course, is the point: Prison had pulled the humanity out of him. Mailer understood that and sought to amplify that critique. He was pugnacious. When reporters accused him of being an enabler of murder, he pushed back, decrying prisons for creating people like Abbott. I could never do that. When anonymous critics began excoriating me online, I went to church.

Not since I was thirteen, getting ready to receive my first communion, had I felt so completely bone-weak. Familiar prayers blurred into unfamiliar tones. The place I always found comforting now felt cavernous. Though it was warm in the sanctuary and the faces around me were welcoming, I felt cold and alone. When we were directed to stand and file out of the pew for communion, I wobbled, knees shaking, and detoured away from the altar to kneel and light a votive.

I watched the thing flicker, praying in questions that I could not answer. Why did Andre do it? What signs did I miss? What more could I have done? I closed my eyes and felt myself floating. I was no longer in the church but directly above the jail, watching myself from outside myself. I could see the speck of me crossing the parking lot, entering the lobby, going through the metal detector, handing over my ID, waiting for the big metal door to grind open so that I could go and sit in Redemption Chapel and wait for the guys.

I was still dazed from church when Terence showed up at my house a few hours later. I had forgotten that we'd made plans to visit Pastor Otis Smith, who runs a recovery home in Church Hill. Pastor Smith and Terence had been with me in class that night when Andre shared his story. I had invited Smith to meet Andre and Terence, and my students. Terence had long wanted to start his own peer recovery service for ex-offenders. He struck up a conversation with Smith after class. The three of us then made arrangements to visit on Sunday and learn more about his reentry program.

Smith greeted us from the front porch of the home with a broad grin but put it away when he saw our faces. I was on the verge of tearing up again. On the car ride over, Terence had been shifting back and forth between a loud wail and a quiet kind of prayer. I was not sure which was coming next. I told Smith the news. He nodded briefly and brought us into the home.

We sat at a card table near a bookshelf stuffed with black binders labeled with topics for sermons or study: faith, work, love, sin. Pastor Smith shifted in his folding chair to move closer to us. His voice slid into a whisper.

"My brothers," he began. "I did not know Andre like you did, but I know what he's been through and what you are going through." He sat back and looked at us one by one. "I was once like Andre. But then I came out of the darkness. I met Jesus in prison. His grace was there with me." He reached for one of the binders—the one labeled sin.

"I can speak on that," Terence said. Pastor Smith smiled as if he had been waiting for exactly this moment and was pleased that it had come sooner rather than later.

"Go on, brother."

"I don't want to preach, now," Terence said. It seemed like he did.

"It's a dialogue," Smith said. "Just a dialogue, my brother. We're talking about saving men from sin."

Terence began to tell his story about his own time praying for deliverance in prison. As he spoke, Smith opened the binder. Then he read the story about Jesus in the desert, denying himself the comforts and false illusions that the devil offered. His chair squeaked beneath him as he gestured with one hand while turning the laminated pages with the other. The radiator knocked behind me.

"Real strength comes from resisting temptation," Smith concluded. "Then comes the redemption." I stopped listening. If heroin—or committing robbery to get money for heroin—was Andre's temptation, shouldn't we at least mention where his taste for that temptation came from? It seemed reductive, a little cruel even, to expect a man to shoulder the whole burden of something that someone forced onto his back as a child.

Pastor Smith came to the wake. It was held at a funeral parlor in Jackson Ward. I took a seat by Shakelia, the woman who had introduced me to Andre when she was still working at the jail. She was crying, rocking her baby. I asked Shakelia why she thought Andre had done it. She handed her baby over to Anton, who had also taken the class at the jail, but who stopped coming sometime after Shakelia formed a relationship with him and was subsequently fired.

"He couldn't sit down," she said as she recalled Andre visiting her and Anton, and their son, Anton Jr., at his first birthday party. "He came. But he just couldn't sit down." Anton picked up where she left off.

"He was restless, Dr. Coogan! He'd be like, 'Anton, we're gonna apply for new jobs tomorrow. C'mon!' And I'd say, why Dre? We have jobs. And he'd say, 'But these here make twenty-five cents more!' And I was like, shoot! Why do we need to run all around for that?" Good question, I thought. Why? "He was always like that. Just always moving. No sooner had we gotten those new jobs than he'd call again. 'Anton, we're going to apply at J. Sargeant Reynolds. We're going back to school.'" Anton shook his head. He couldn't understand that constant movement.

I left town. But I could not enjoy Christmas in my childhood home in Connecticut. The tree was in the same spot. My father was opening a bottle of wine. The children were making gingerbread cookies for Santa with Nonna. My mind kept drifting back to Richmond. A lawyer who read the news story about Andre had sent a letter to the dean of my school, demanding that I be fired. I was going up for tenure that year. My file was in the dean's office. The unpublished manuscript that would become *Writing Our Way Out* featured prominently in the application.

When I got back to Richmond, I was summoned to the dean's office. We sat at the small round table by his desk. He opened my file and began to page through it. In addition to the material that I had submitted, the file contained reports from committees that had evaluated my teaching, scholarship, and service. Though I had not seen the reports, I knew that each one ended with a recommendation to grant or deny tenure. It was now up to the dean to interpret the reports and make a decision before sending the file to the provost, who would send it to the president, who would send it to the board of visitors. Typically, each committee rubber-stamped the previous committee's recommendation. For all of the formality to the process, the dean's decision was essentially the final decision.

"David," he began slowly, carefully, as if he were just now emerging from a much longer cogitation. "You must have known before you began teaching prisoners that there would be some risks?" He closed the file in slow motion and looked up. His blue eyes were large behind rimless glasses. Risks? I suppose I had considered them, but I was more focused on what I was gaining than what I could lose. Now I had lost Andre. And I was sad. But I was wary of letting my guard down to grieve when my name had been linked to a front-page crime story. I was angry at the police for the high-speed chase and at Andre for the robbery. I thought he had changed, but now I doubted my ability to recognize change. Was this crime a one-time event, or was it yet another among the dozens of robberies that he had talked his way out of in court? Had he been deceiving me the whole time? Was that the risk that I had taken? Taking him at his word?

"But you knew it was the right thing to do," I heard the dean answering his own question. I nodded again, feigning the confidence that I did not feel. He stood. I stood. Then we were smiling, shaking hands, strolling to the front door. He patted me on the back and handed me the file. I clutched it, feeling furtive, and walked into the chill of winter. Snowflakes filled a cerulean sky. People passing by had no idea. Nobody knew! Andre was dead, and I had a job for life.

Tell me, what else should I have done?
Doesn't everything die at last, and too soon?
Tell me, what is it you plan to do
with your one wild and precious life?—Mary Oliver[19]

On that summer day, Mary Oliver knelt in a field to feed sugar to a grasshopper. She knew—maybe then, maybe later when she wrote the poem—that it would die. But she wanted to help it live. What else should I have done, kneeling in the fields of Andre's life, offering the only words I had?

10
Hero

Dave

Spring, 2010. Rejection had become routine. There was evasive reasoning. Platitudes about taste. Shoulder shrugs about the book market. A general wariness of books by prisoners. Still, every Saturday, I went to my office and entered into the ritual of sending my book proposal to literary agents and reading their rejections. On one of those sad Saturdays, the phone rang. It startled me. The phone never rang. The only people who knew I was here were the guys and my wife.

"David Coogan?"

"Yes?"

"Hi. Yeah, it's Walter. You just emailed your proposal. I was going to write again, but then I thought, nah, I should call." This was my second time pitching the book to Walter. Unlike the other agents, who sent form letter rejections, he actually wrote to explain that, while he liked the premise of a writing class in a jail, he wanted more scenes of me teaching it. At that time, the manuscript was an anthology of memoirs from the guys, with an introduction by me. After Walter's first email rejection, I tried to rewrite it with more scenes from the class dispersed throughout.

"I'm sorry, David, but I can't accept this." His voice was all New York. Yet the website describing his agency said he was in Florida. I imagined him semi-retired down there. The fronds of palm trees shimmering outside his kitchen window, coffee going cold as he read proposals on his computer, wondering which one would send him back to New York.

"What's the problem?"

"You're not the hero."

"What?"

"You've got to be the one changing them."

I looked at the snapshots of the guys on my bulletin board. I remembered forming this collective that produced this manuscript he was rejecting: Kelvin in a grey track suit, sitting by my desk with a green pen and a grin; Ronald, Dean, and Terence at Richmond Hill, a Christian retreat center, at an event that we held for at-risk kids from a local high school; Stan in a tan uniform in Redemption Chapel at the jail, where we had the class. I lingered on the photo of Andre in prison reds tacked next to the memorial card that I had saved from his wake.

"But I didn't change anyone," I heard myself saying in a small voice.

"Look," he said, mouth closer to the receiver now. "I can't go to New York, ride all the way up that elevator, walk into some editor's office, jump up and down, and say, 'You've got to buy this book!' if you're not the hero." I felt the walls closing in on me. All of the classes, all of the letters, all of the visits to prison, all of the meetings with the guys after prison—all of that oxygen we had breathed into the project, together, in a spirit of trust and support, was getting shrink-wrapped into a hero story.

"The book is not about me. And if you talk to anyone who has taught in a prison, they'll tell you: The teacher is a focal point, but not the whole focus. The teacher doesn't change anyone." I could hear him breathing. I could sense him considering. Then he started talking about a book he sold to St. Martin's Press: *Picking Cotton: Our Memoir of Injustice and Redemption.*

Ronald Cotton, a Black man in North Carolina, is accused of raping a white woman in her home. The woman, Jennifer Thompson-Cannino, reports the crime and is summoned to the police station to pick the perpetrator out of a lineup. She picks Cotton. He goes to prison. Ten years later, DNA evidence proves his innocence, and Thompson-Cannino testifies that she had been coerced by the detectives to pick someone, anyone, from that lineup. Cotton is exonerated. And the two of them form an unlikely friendship after the trial. With a ghostwriter, they tell their story.[20]

If a hero is an honorable person who triumphs over adversity, this book has two: Cotton, who endures prison and is freed, and Thompson-Cannino, who endures rape and the guilt of sending an innocent man to prison, but who is able to help set the record straight. It is a powerful story. But as I tried explaining to the agent, who was not my agent, most Black men in prison are not likely to be saved at a jury trial with DNA evidence and the dramatic reversal of key testimony from the victim. Most are not in prison for rape or murder. They're in for possession. Or possession with the intent to distribute. Robbery. Larceny. An unlicensed gun. That kind of thing.

"Their stories are not really about crime but about the internal drama that led to the crime." A few beats passed as he processed what I was saying.

"Like *Dangerous Minds*," he said at last. "Or *Freedom Writers*. That's more recent. Have you seen those films?" I had. Beautiful white women find themselves teaching Black and brown kids in inner-city high schools rife with violence, gangs, and puberty. "Like that," he concluded. "We need to see you . . ."

"Saving Black people?" I interrupted.

"Woah," he chuckled, a little surprised. "I don't make the rules. That's just how these stories go." We entered into another pause, our last one. There was nowhere else to go.

I hung up the phone, stood, and began pacing the small space of the office. The air was stale. I felt a strange longing for the academic presses I had left behind. I missed their proud devotion to the disciplines, their transparent criteria for submitting manuscripts, their wordy websites with instructions and contact information, and, most of all, their indifference to all of those eyeballs bobbing out there in the sea of the "general reader." The problem was that the academic presses I had approached didn't know what to make of the manuscript either. They did not want a manuscript featuring the writings from a class in jail. They wanted advice on how to teach writing in a jail or an argument about what was wrong with the criminal justice system.

I had a Goldilocks problem. The manuscript was too hot for academic presses, but too cold for agents. It was too much story to impress scholars, but not enough of a white savior story to fly off airport bookstore shelves. Of course, I thought the manuscript was just right. The problem was not with the manuscript but with these gatekeepers of manuscripts. I needed to talk with someone who knew the commercial book business.

David Robbins is one of the few people I know who makes a living publishing fiction. When I told him about my manuscript problem, he told me to send it to him so he could read it and figure it out. He called back the next week and invited me to go sailing. We could talk about it as we sailed. Once the schooner left the harbor, I dug into the agent's claim that I needed to be more of a hero. David listened while trimming the mainsail. When I had finished complaining, he politely disagreed.

"The guy said hero." He shrugged and offered a small wince. "What he really meant was guide. He was trying to tell you to be a stronger narrator." I steadied myself on the port bench.

"The book is not about me."

"It is, though," he said. I stared back, unconvinced. "It's commendable, what you did, getting them to open up. It would make a good story." His eyes were on the telltales. When they lifted, he pushed the tiller. The sail snapped. The hull lurched. I grabbed the rail behind me to stop from sliding down the bench.

"That's not the story I'm trying to tell."

"Look, I read what you sent me. I wasn't interested in Stan getting adopted. Or Kelvin's mother making fried chicken for lunch. None of that. I was interested in why you care about them." We hit some swells. I sought out the horizon. I needed a fixed point to steady myself and push down a creeping nausea. "Readers of memoir need to be able to slip into your story. They need to get past the membrane separating their world from yours." He stopped speaking to consider me.

"Maybe you're not the kind of guy who writes a memoir? Maybe you're too humble?" His voice had softened. He had figured me out. I got up and went to sit in the bow. Sun sparked the sea. Waves sloshed against the hull. I saw the roofline of a port town up ahead. I leaned back against the cabin and closed my eyes. I saw the same outline of that roofline in the orange of my eyelids. Why did readers need me to be their guide? Why couldn't the guys speak for themselves?

I reconsidered that stance when I read Mark Salzman's *True Notebooks: A Writer's Year at Juvenile Hall,* which tells a compelling story of him teaching a writing class in prison. Like my manuscript, it features the writings of the boys from his class. But unlike my manuscript at that time, he blends his story of teaching the class with the boys' writings in a way that shows both his own development as a protagonist and the boys' dilemmas in the criminal justice system. In my letter to his publisher, I thanked Mark for the book and let him know I planned to use it in my prison literature class. I told him about the book I was writing, sent a few chapters, and asked if he thought his editor at Vintage might like to read it.

A month later, he wrote via email, thanking me for the letter but saying he doubted he would have much influence at Vintage. Compared with his novels, he explained, Vintage considered *True Notebooks* a financial disappointment. It had not sold twenty-five thousand copies in a year.

Twenty-five thousand copies! I couldn't believe what I was reading. I had never taken the time to think through what a big publisher might expect in terms of sales. Money is an unreality in academic publishing, at least in my experience. Money doesn't figure into the motivation to publish or the spoils for having published. It is barely discussed in the book contracts.

Mark concluded that while he could not help me with Vintage, he knew a guy in LA who might be able to help with HarperCollins: His friend, Joe Loya, who had recently published a memoir, *The Man Who Outgrew His Prison Cell: Confessions of a Bank Robber*. Joe was unknown to publishers before that book, he explained. If he could get HarperCollins interested, maybe he could coach me on how to do it? Mark made the introduction, forwarding my letter to Joe. A week or so later, I got a call.

"Mark tells me you need advice on publishing." His voice was melodious, a little mischievous.

"Yes. Thanks for calling." I heard a dull but consistent hum of voices around him.

"All right, player. Let's do this. I'm on line at Starbucks. Pitch."

"Oh, okay. Well, it's about this writing class I started at the jail. It's about each guy's struggle to figure out how he got caught up and how he can stay out." There was a bit of a lull as he considered the premise.

"You're an English professor?"

"Yes."

"You're probably thinking of citing Foucault."

"It's more of a memoir than an argument."

"But you're thinking about it."

"Maybe?"

"Well, stop thinking about it!"

"Okay."

"Save that for your journals."

"Got it."

"Caramel macchiato! Double shot! Extra whip! You got a proposal?"

"Yeah."

"How long is it?"

"About fifteen pages."

"Woah, WOAH! Slow down, chief! Should be seven to ten."

I asked if he would be willing to read a revised proposal and sample chapter. He agreed. A few weeks later, he called again. He had spotted some key things that he could fix . . . for a fee.

"What kind of things?"

"It's hard to explain over the phone."

"Maybe you could send a few pages so I can see for myself. A sample. No charge?"

"Gratis," he said softly, almost in a hiss.

His edits were good. But I was not so frustrated that I was willing to pay someone to solve my problem. Also, after reflecting back on my conversation, it occurred to me that Joe Loya did not get a book contract with HarperCollins because of his writing ability alone. It was those cojones. The same ones he used to rob all those banks.

* * *

"Yes!" I blurted. I was walking to campus, looking at my phone. An old guy in front of me turned around to stare. I didn't care. How could he know that I had just gotten an email from Michelle Alexander, the bestselling author of *The New Jim Crow: Mass Incarceration in the Age of Colorblindness?* Hers was the book that made criminal justice reform suddenly urgent and everywhere in the media in 2010. I had sent her a letter with our book proposal and the sample chapters in care of her publisher, The New Press. That was eight months ago. She apologized for her delayed response. She was just now getting a break from her book tour and was overwhelmed by all the mail she'd gotten. She did not have time to respond to it all, but she was drawn to my letter and manuscript.

She commended me for helping the people whose lives had been caught up in that disastrous policy. She did not have time to write an introduction, as I had asked, but she agreed that, yes, I should consider sending my manuscript to her editor, Elaine, at The New Press. I wrote to Elaine the next day. Then I forced myself to wait patiently for her response. After a month, I decided to follow up with a call.

I closed the office door and stared at the phone. I relaxed my shoulders, took a deep breath, and let it out. I practiced my lines silently. Then, I practiced them aloud. I squirmed in my chair, stood and stretched, then sat down again. Okay, I said to myself. I am just going to do this. I am going to call Elaine at the New Press. I am going to ask what she thought of the proposal and sample chapters that I sent. I'm going to ask her if she is ready to see the whole manuscript. I punched in the number. The line gurgled. Abruptly, a young woman answered.

"The New Press. How may I direct your call?"

"To Elaine."

"And who is calling?"

"Dave Coogan."

"Okay, just a minute." I listened to the office noise. I imagined the building. I knew it was near Wall Street. I had been to New York many times as a tourist. I wondered what it would be like to go there on business. I would go whenever she wanted me to go. I would take the train tomorrow if she wanted me to. I would . . .

"Who is this?" Elaine barked. I sprang from my chair and began pacing as far as the grey cord allowed. Her tone told me she was in no mood—and was not likely to be in the mood anytime soon—to speak with someone she did not know. I had a few minutes, at best, to keep her from hanging up on me. I segued from my name to Michelle Alexander's name and explained that Michelle, her bestselling author, had suggested I send her my manuscript. Michelle's book, I explained, makes the argument against mass incarceration. Mine offers memoirs from the people impacted by it. It would make a great follow-up for readers coming to The New Press for titles about mass incarceration.

"Did I ask for this?" She had not. But Michelle Alexander, I said once more, shifting my weight from left to right, winding my words up to release the pitch again.

"Look, you're going about this all wrong. Getting a book contract like this is old-fashioned. Start a Twitter account. Go on YouTube. Make a name for yourself. THEN come back and ask for a book contract." I puzzled over the idea that social media could drive publishing; that publishing did not create publicity but needed publicity like a kind of fuel; that editors and agents were more powerful than the authors they published.

"Okay, I'll do that. Thank you."

"Yeah, sure," she said, with a hint of contempt. I heard her scolding the intern for interrupting her before the line went dead.

I decided I needed to visit Stan. It was late in the morning when I finally got to Greensville Correctional Center. From Richmond, the drive was just about an hour, but the waiting and processing to get into the visiting room added another few hours. Stan wore dark blue jeans and a light-blue collared shirt open at the neck. He had no jewelry or sunglasses, but his smooth gait and trim hair gave him the appearance of leisure. I stood when he arrived at my scuffed plastic table. Then he winded me with a bro hug and hearty back slap.

"Thanks for coming, man! For real." I caught my breath, smiled, and showed him a ziplock bag full of coins.

"What do you want?"

"It don't matter. Anything sweet."

I stood in line. The vending machines were lit up like slot machines. The microwaves beeped like semitrucks backing up. Two little boys were leaning into each other in a competition to see who would fall out of line first. Ahead of them was an older Black man who looked like he had just come from church. Ahead of him was a young Black woman in clothes tight enough to catch her man's eye but not so revealing that she would be disallowed from visiting hours. A white woman with a choppy haircut was feeding quarters into the lips of the drink machine. Eventually, I returned to Stan with two honey buns and two Cokes.

"How's the book coming?" he asked as he opened the soda. I sighed and told him all about the phone call with the former bank robber, the boat ride with the novelist, and my brush with the celebrated public intellectual Michelle Alexander.

"I can't always tell if I'm making any progress."

"Yeah," he said as he ripped open the honey bun.

"It's taking a while, too."

"It's all good, Dave. I appreciate it. We all appreciate what you're doing."

"Thanks, Stan. I don't mind telling you, I poured a stiff drink after that talk with the bank robber."

"You'd have to! Got to take the edge off!"

"And then there was this agent I talked with over the phone. He kept trying to convince me the book needed a hero."

"Hmm." Stan chewed, cocking his head to the side and cracking his neck. He swallowed and winced like he'd just tasted something sour. "I look at it like this, right? Our stories are *okay*. But it's your determination to hear our stories that will make it a good book."

I set my Coke down and sat back. He was saying the same thing as Walter. The same thing as David.

"Listen, man," Stan continued. "I wouldn't be publishing a book if it weren't for you. None of us would."

Something started to settle into place for me then. Stan was using different words, but he was essentially saying that because I was their guide in the writing class, I could be the guide in the book, too. It felt different, though, hearing it from him.

On the highway back to Richmond, I listened to *Car Talk*. A woman joked with the loveable brother mechanics from Boston that her husband was forever complaining about her highway driving. He said she made too many jerky movements. But *he* was the one who waited too long to correct course, veering into the next lane before straightening out! She knew how to bend with the road. The brothers agreed with her assessment. It was radio banter, but I heard in it a kind of prophecy. I had not gone to jail to write a book. I had gone to teach a writing class. As to what would come of those writings, I had only imagined a kind of zine or class project cranked out over some Xerox machine. But the road of our project was bending. I had to bend with it. I had to correct course.

When Kelvin came to the office the next week to work on his resume, I updated him on my visit with Stan and my progress on the book. If it was ever going to get published, I admitted, I was going to have to write more of myself into it.

"The problem is that I don't know what to write. I don't think I really have a story," I confessed.

"Dave!" he blurted my name like an accusation. "Let me break this down for you, okay? I've done a lot of time. I've seen a lot of volunteers. And I can tell you: People don't come into the jail like you did, asking so many damn questions and really listening to what we have to say. You may not see it, but I'm telling you. You're unusual for a volunteer."

That sent me back in memory. I remembered all those times walking across the parking lot to the front door of the jail, into the lobby, through the metal detector, and up to the dirty plastic window where I surrendered my ID and clipped the visitor badge to my collar. I'd wait for the big metal door to grind open, then wait again at the bars worn smooth from hands like mine, gripping them while listening for the buzz that triggered the lock that snapped like a bear trap and always caught my heart. I only had a split second to pull the door open. Many times, I missed it. But I was determined to get in.

"It's your curiosity!" Kelvin said at last. "That's unusual."

11
A Constant State of Rage

Naji

Coming home from the penitentiary in 2008 was a culture shock, to say the least. By writing my memoirs in the last book, I was reawakened to the trauma I experienced as a child: Discovering my mother dead when I was just a kid, getting adopted by my grandmother who beat me whenever she could, all the put-downs and emotional abuse. Although the process was therapeutic, it was also retraumatizing. Realizing that my dysfunction could be due to unresolved issues rooted in child abuse fucked me up! I remember thinking, Who am I? More importantly, who could I have been? I felt cheated. I was grateful for the awakening, but I was angry. I didn't deserve this shit! Internally, I struggled to understand Allah's plan. I needed answers.

As human beings, the most important thing we can ever seek to know in this world is who and what we are. I don't think there's anything more necessary. This understanding becomes the catalyst, the divine spark from which we navigate our physical environment and understand the meaning of life. To be aware is to be alive.

My grandfather passed while I was incarcerated. So now the gatekeeper was my grandmother. She was the only one who could answer the most important question that seemed to be tearing a hole in my very soul: *Why?* How should I approach the subject? Should I let loose the anger inside me? Should I cuss her out?

Allah asks us to be humble and mindful of him in situations like this. Surely there must be exceptions! Why do I need to be respectful of my grandmother? My whole life has been fucked up because my grandmother decided that I was to be treated like a piece of shit. Internally, I was going through it! At the same time, my efforts at deep introspection and educating myself had a surprising side effect.

I had become socially conscious in a way that put me in direct conflict with everything I thought I knew about myself and the world. Concepts such as racism, colonialism, and nationalism had become a part of my knowledge base. My view of the world was slowly becoming a worldview.

I felt like Neo after choosing the red pill. The world I thought I understood had become dark and extremely hostile. The more I studied, the more I saw myself as part of an ethnicity with no cultural identity. On top of that, not knowing myself as a person left me completely fractured. The enormity of putting Humpty Dumpty back together again seemed almost impossible.

James Baldwin said, "To be a negro in this country and to be relatively conscious is to be in a state of rage almost all of the time." Forced conformity to the social norms of a group that for hundreds of years has based the idea of themselves, in practice and through silence, on the inferiority of African people in this country and all over the world has handicapped, retarded, and socially incapacitated me and my people. I was broken. And understandably so. It was crystal clear that I needed to question everything I had learned—I had to decolonize my very thoughts. I was absolutely lost in this world, entering kindergarten as a middle-aged man. How depressing is that? Little did I know how deep the rabbit hole descended.

With this colossal weight on my shoulders, with this unquenchable thirst for an objective reality, I was released from prison back into the cultural cesspool. I went straight to the home I was raised in. I wanted to surprise my grandmother, but in a normal way. I was somewhat excited to see her, and I figured she would feel, in some way, the same. Our relationship was far more complicated than I had realized. It was about to get even more so.

While incarcerated, through many hours of self-reflection, I had become aware of the depth of my dysfunction. Contemplating release and having the opportunity to confront my grandparents about their treatment of my mother, my siblings, and me became my primary focus. It wasn't anger that drove me, but a deep need to explain why I had become this person.

My whole life had consisted of teachers, counselors, prosecutors, jailers, and wardens telling me that I was smart, but because I had decided to be a criminal, I deserved no mercy or compassion. Now I could stop the self-blame, contempt, and hatred I felt for myself and lay the responsibility, at least to some degree, where it rightly belonged. Imagine the questions you would have, the desire you would feel to see contrition in your abuser's eyes. Maybe even a sincere verbal apology, or a tear that would reveal genuine regret and remorse. The simple acknowledgement that they had wronged me would mean the world!

I showed up at my grandmother's house unannounced in an attempt to surprise her. My excitement and anticipation levels were through the roof! I knocked on the door, the door swung open, and I found myself staring at an unfamiliar face. A short, brown, older woman smiled at me and asked if she could help me. I said yes, ma'am, my name is Naji, and this is my grandmother's house. Could you please have her come to the door? I had no idea who this woman was or what she was doing in my grandmother's house.

She invited me inside. As soon as my foot crossed the threshold, I knew something was terribly wrong. My grandmother was known for keeping an immaculate home. She was obsessed with it. I couldn't count the many ass whoopings I'd received growing up for wrinkling a rug or moving something out of place. I would later learn that my grandmother suffered from, among other things, OCD.

What I was seeing was a living room that was dark and gloomy. The stench of mildew was thick in the air. The curtains were dingy, and even though the sun was shining bright, they let in little light. Two small children sat on the couch staring at me as if I were the one out of place. I instantly got an uncomfortable feeling in the pit of my stomach.

"Who are you?" I asked. "And where is my grandmother?"

She explained that she was my brother's wife and that she had been taking care of my grandmother for the last few months. Being that my brother is incarcerated with a life sentence, I really didn't understand the dynamics of this relationship or what deal had been struck in order for her to be present in my grandmother's house. She told me my grandmother was in her bedroom, so I rushed back to see her, now more concerned for her welfare than about any reckoning I had planned.

At the entrance to her bedroom, the first thing I noticed was a shadow hanging from the ceiling, just floating in the air. As I got closer, I realized I was looking at a spider web, one that crossed over her bed from one corner of the room to the other. Attached to the web were clumps of dust that hung like stalactites in a cave. Beneath it was my grandmother, who seemed so focused on some TV show on her outdated black-and-white, she didn't even realize I was there.

I scanned the room and was shocked at its cluttered condition. My grandmother appeared emaciated. Her skin was dehydrated and scaly. She wore a flowery white nightgown that was stained yellow and brown. I couldn't fathom what I was seeing!

"Hey, Grandma," I said. She looked up at me, squinting. Her expression indicated that she didn't recognize me. My mind reeled. "It's me, Naji." Her face contorted into a look of disbelief, her mouth twisting to one corner of her face

"You're David," she rattled, referencing my older brother, who had been incarcerated for the last seven years. "I know who you are."

"Grandma, it's me," I replied, bewildered. I moved to the foot of the bed so she could have a clear view of me. "It's me, Grandma. I was just released today." As she studied my face, I began to think she was just in shock: She hadn't seen me for so long that she couldn't believe I was standing before her. Further inspection revealed to me that she really didn't know who I was. After a couple of seconds of looking at me, her eyes glanced back over to the TV, and she became silent and involved in her show once again.

I stepped to the side of her bed and pulled back the covers. I wanted to see if her legs and feet were in the same condition as her hands, arms, and face. A frenzy of dark blotches scrambled in all directions. They crawled over her legs and lap, seeking safety in the dark recesses of her covers. It must have been twenty or thirty roaches. She was completely unaware and unaffected. Crumbs from all types of food—cookies, potato chips, cake crumbs—littered the spot where she lay. I looked down and was appalled to see her toenails had grown out over the tips of her toes and were curling back under them!

"What the fuck!" My head began to throb. My heart raced. Adrenaline surged through my veins. I was becoming angry to the point of distraction. My eyes landed on the open bags of potato chips, cookies, and other junk food piled to the side of her bed. I immediately wanted to know what other food she'd been eating. Not much, based on her appearance. I rushed to the kitchen, passing the strangers seated in the living room. I yanked open the refrigerator. Inside was a half-eaten hot dog, a quarter of a bottle of mayonnaise, some ketchup, and someone's half-eaten Subway sandwich, partially opened and thrown haphazardly on a shelf. I opened the freezer and discovered that ice had accumulated all around the inside to the point that there was maybe enough room to stick your hand in the middle. A barely visible open bag of peas stuck out from one of the ice-encrusted walls.

I slammed the door and went into the living room. I asked the lady, my brother's wife, why the house and my grandmother were in such a sorry state. She looked at me as if she didn't understand the issue. I asked her how long she had been there. She told me she was my grandmother's caretaker and that she was there to make sure she had a bath, ate, and was taken care of.

"Lady, when's the last time she had a bath? When was the last time she ate a meal? Why are there roaches in the bed with her and cobwebs hanging from the ceiling? Bags of junk food and trash around her bed? How the hell can you claim that you've been taking care of her?"

Not waiting for her response, I told her to get her kids, pack up her shit, and move it out of my grandmother's house ASAP. I was on the brink of losing my mind! I could not believe that anyone would do this to an elderly person, especially my grandmother. When she didn't move fast enough, I began grabbing her stuff and throwing it out the front door. Within an hour, everything she owned was at the curb.

She called the police on me, thinking that because I was just released, I was somehow in violation, and she could have me locked up again. In turn, she almost went to jail for elder abuse. I packed my grandmother's house up, cleaned it out, changed the locks on the doors, took the key to the rental office, and relocated my grandmother to Arizona. I was still on probation in Virginia, but I got that transferred to Arizona. I would still have to report. But I needed to get off the East Coast. My ex-wife was in Arizona, the one who spoke for me in court years ago, but who left me when my addiction resurfaced. So that was part of what drew me there. But I also thought changing the people, places, and things I was accustomed to would suffice in changing my life, not realizing that the problem was within me, and I took it with me wherever I went.

On the plane ride, I had the opportunity to reflect on what I had just experienced. It occurred to me that my need to get answers from my grandmother had taken a back seat to a strong protective feeling, like a parent, I imagine, would have for their offspring. I was not mad. I did have trauma-associated feelings, and I wanted answers, but at this point, it was clear to me that Allah had touched my heart, and forgiveness flowed through me. I instinctively understood the opportunity for growth. I began acting as a loving grandson, no more, no less.

It was very difficult for me to accept that I could not get the answers I was looking for. I felt that with that knowledge would come a deeper understanding of who I was as a person, and this would help guide me toward some kind of peace and closure. It was never to be. My grandmother suffered from dementia that only got worse until she passed in 2009.

During the time I spent caring for her before she passed, I would often reflect on the reversal of circumstances. Here I was, the victim, taking care of my victimizer. There were times I would broach the subject with her, praying for a moment of lucidity, only to get the same look of bewilderment and confusion.

Eventually, I realized I needed to share my experience of dealing with trauma and addiction. I decided to pursue a new career as a drug counselor. I procured a job as a home health care aide to my grandmother, and since I would be working from home, I enrolled in online classes at Rio Salado Community College in Tempe. In no time, I was at the top of my class, but I was unequipped to handle the amount of stress that came with all of the new responsibilities I'd undertaken. Soon, my addiction reared its head, and I began to drink beer on occasion. I never realized how the stress of my relationship, my grandmother, bills, and lack of immediate family support contributed to my desire to use. It crept up on me like a black ant, on a black rock, in the darkest of nights. I really didn't think it would go any further than just drinking beer occasionally, but gradually over time, I picked up my drug of choice, which was cocaine.

Cocaine is an ugly drug. You quickly become a slave to its influence, and you find yourself unable to properly conduct your life without it. But of course, any life with it is tragic. Everything suffers: relationships, finances, social interactions, spiritual connections. You become isolated from the mainstream world and hide from the light of day.

Following my grandmother's passing, I had moved in with my ex-wife, but our relationship began to crumble. I wasn't the only one at fault, but I played a major part. I wasn't strong enough to address the issues we were having, and so they became major problems. Fueled by my addiction, I began to feel as I did when I was a child. Home became the last place I wanted to be. The stress and constant arguing provided an excuse to venture away from my relationship. With all the progress I made while incarcerated, I still had not matured to the level where I could handle the type of stress and depression I was facing. I didn't know how to articulate to my ex-wife exactly how I was feeling, so I became extremely lonely and isolated.

At no time in my life after losing my first love, Cassandra, did I stop thinking about her. Cassandra was my high school sweetheart. She knew my story better than anyone. It sounds crass, but honestly, my love for her was eternal, no matter who I was with. Eventually, my ex-wife caught me communicating on social media with the true love of my life. We had a big falling out. She concocted a lie that I was selling drugs and that I was a threat to her. She contacted my probation officer and requested that I be removed from the home we shared. My name was on the lease, but as it turned out, that didn't matter. I was ordered to leave the house. With nowhere to go, I was forced to leave everything behind: my laptop, artwork, and supplies, everything but my clothes, which my ex brought to the probation office and dropped off at the door. She purposely kept everything she knew held meaning to me. I was destroyed!

I found myself homeless and at odds with the probation office. I had no family or friends in Arizona. I was completely alone. I reached out to the only family I knew, the family who was always there for me, no matter what, the streets. Of course, my addiction escalated considerably. I was completely out of control. Oddly, I had been enrolled in college to study chemical dependency counseling, but being on the streets with no computer and trying to navigate social resources for food, clothing, and shelter was next to impossible.

Every morning, I would wake up early and take the bus to Arizona State University to use their computer lab for my online classes. I was doing so well, at the top of my class, and despite my issues with drugs, it was really important to me to finish. But I was dragging myself. I couldn't maintain. Intellectually, I was fine. But emotionally, I was stressed. This became another source of depression because I really believed furthering my education would help me make something better of my life.

I was now awash in a sea of doubt, self-pity, and depravity. It wasn't apparent to me that my actions and thought processes were the cause of all the hell I was going through. My life had taught me to see myself as a victim, and the defeatist mentality that accompanies that view of the world had settled in deeply. I could see no way out.

12
The Builder

Dave

Spring, 2010. The lobby of the jail looked just the way I left it. Dirty linoleum. Painted cinder block. Scratched-up window with the silver intercom that only lets out a voice. To speak back to the deputy, you have to lean down and put your face in front of the slot. I did not need to do that today. John Dooley, the jail's director of education, was here to guide me.

He looked like a farmer called in from the fields, impatient to be sitting when there was work to be done back there. His shirt was blue, checkered, untucked, and enormous. He had no badge, handcuffs, or walkie-talkie, just a ring of gold skeleton keys and a creased piece of paper. Though seated, his head was just about eye-level when I stood before him.

"Are you ready?" he asked in a low, resonant voice. He stood, and we moved to the steel door separating the lobby from the jail. When the door slid open, he gestured for me to go first. A chalky light filled the long hall. A walkie-talkie choked on its own static. We approached the bars. A buzzer sounded to trigger the lock, and I flinched with the muscle memory of the many times I'd missed my chance to pull the door open. John's heavily tattooed arm moved quickly, grabbing the top bar well beyond my reach.

We passed Redemption Chapel, where I used to teach the class and where I met John by chance in the spring of 2007. He'd been surprised to see a volunteer on a Saturday. He was even more surprised when I told him I was from the university and that I had been teaching writing here since last summer. He'd been teaching at the jail for thirty-some years, he told me, and no one from any of the nearby universities had come to volunteer more than a handful of times. I asked him what he taught. He said GED, but when he explained the class, it sounded more like poetry. He invited me to come visit the school during the week. Anytime, he explained. Just come in and tell the deputies to call him. He would come get me.

His offer to come teach during the week was appealing. I was getting tired of giving up my Saturdays. And the class that I had begun was coming to an end. At that time, in the spring of 2007, only Stan and Kelvin were left from the original class. I had not planned on teaching people in jail indefinitely. By the end of that spring, I had ended the class at the jail.

Three years had passed. It was now 2010. Dean, Ronald, Kelvin, Naji, and Terence were all out. Andre was dead. The others were still in prison, writing me letters. The process of finding a publisher for the book was ongoing. I had faith that I would find one. I just did not know when. What could I do while I was waiting? I wanted to make teaching at the jail a regular part of my job. Maybe John could help. Maybe I did not have to go on doing this work alone.

We moved slowly down the hall. John's stride was ursine. He stuck a skeleton key into a side door and wound it around. It clicked open like a safe. On the landing of the stairwell, he smiled a little, then locked the door behind him. He seemed more at ease now that we were away from the lobby. At the bottom of the stairs, he opened yet another heavy door, let me through, and locked it behind us. When we entered the basement, it struck me that I had never really seen the jail. Just the chapel near the lobby. As we walked, we talked about books. Touchstones for teaching. Literature that lends itself to an understanding of what people are going through in prison. He recommended *The Snow Leopard* by Peter Matthiessen. Later, I started reading it to understand the one recommending it.

"This place . . ." John said, shaking his head. There was a drip underneath one of the exposed water pipes in the basement, and a bucket under the drip. Someone had tried to stop it with tape. We arrived at the school. He flipped through the ring of keys.

"The fellas are ready for you," he said. "Lots of writing to share." I nodded, imagining them in there already, but when he opened the door, the room was empty. Long tables lined the wall with neat stacks of textbooks in front of outdated computers. A fisherman's net was pinned to the ceiling, sagging in places under the weight of large shells. The walls were covered with homemade poems, artwork, and posters.

"I'll be right back," John said. "Just going up upstairs to get the men." I nodded. "I have to lock the door for security." I nodded again. "You'll be safe." I hadn't considered that I would not. The door closed. I heard the key twisting. Then I was alone.

I wandered the school like a museum, studying the larger posters. Gandhi radiating wisdom. Che Guevara smoldering in his beret. Mother Teresa looking off to the side, praying. Jimmy Santiago Baca flashing a Cheshire Cat grin. Olympic athletes from 1968 giving the Black Power salute. There were smaller black-and-white printout pictures of Sheriff Woody, the chaplain of the jail, Father Pruitt, and group shots of the students earning their GEDs.

John returned with more men than I thought could fit into the rectangle of an office. The sudden influx of people got my attention. All of the plastic stackable chairs were taken. John introduced me as Dave, an English professor from VCU, the one who had been teaching the writing class in the chapel. They nodded and stared. John turned to go sit at his teacher's desk behind me, warning them casually to pay attention or else.

I told the men about the class that I taught for nine months in the chapel. I talked about writing as a way of learning more about your life and, ideally, figuring out how to make some changes, so that you can stop coming to jail. I told them that I'd like to start another class here. They agreed. A little box filled with golf pencils made its way around the room. I opened my notebook to pull out some writing prompts. A man in the back who looked to be about my age raised his hand. His face was smooth. His voice was soft. When I acknowledged him, he stood to speak with one arm behind his back.

"You said you did this kind of writing class for nine months?"

"Yeah."

"Does it work?"

"What do you mean?"

"Will you be able to read what I write and figure out my problem?" I looked around the room. One guy was poking through a copy of the Diagnostic and Statistical Manual of Mental Disorders.

"Hey, can you hold up that book?" His sculpted, tattooed arm rose like a totem pole and slowly rotated the book. "Can everyone see?" They mumbled yes. "Do you know what that is?" They shook their heads. "That is what therapists use to diagnose your problem." The man lowered the book. "The main difference between a therapist and me is that I don't know what's in that book." They chuckled and exhaled. "I won't be able to tell you your problem. All I can do is teach you how to write about it so that you can figure it out for yourself."

"Ahh!" the man said. "That just makes me trust you all the more!" He stopped speaking, but was not done. He entered into a private reverie, then suddenly returned. When he resumed speaking, his voice had dropped down into a whisper. "You see, I've been around those kinds of people all my life. I *know* what they want from me. And I *know* how to give it to them. But *you*!" He folded his hands in front of him. "I don't *know* what you want! And I like that." He sat down, smiling. The guy next to him smiled and pumped a fist.

"All I want is for you to try. I think every man in here should try to help himself by writing."

"*Real* talk," a man in the middle of the room said under his breath. I leaned in, unsure that I had heard him. "I said that's REAL TALK!"

* * *

The Snow Leopard is not set in prison. Matthiessen is hiking the Himalayas with a zoologist who is searching for blue sheep and, if luck prevails, the elusive snow leopard. Matthiessen is searching for something else, something internal. He is mourning the loss of his wife, who died of cancer earlier that year. He does not come right out and say he is mourning. He simply reports her passing and a little of their history as travelers and seekers of meaning, sometimes induced by LSD (it was the era for it) and books of philosophy. They had children. Most are older and living on their own. But to make this trip to the Himalayas, he leaves his eight-year-old with a network of friends and family. The boy does not want him to go. The few letters that he writes to his father expressing his sadness and anger, and his self-talk to toughen up, are painful.

There is not much plot. The plot is not the point. The chapter titles are the days of the hike. The hike is filled with monotony, mystery, pain, and beauty, sometimes all on the same day. There are "vacant children, listless adults, bent dogs and thin chickens in a litter of sagging shacks and rubble, mud, weeds, stagnant ditches, bad sweet smells, vivid bright broken plastic bits, and dirty fruit peelings awaiting the carrion pig."[21] There are also monsoons, malingering porters, boots full of blood, cold wet tents, cakes of cow dung, snowcapped mountains, and crippled children singing to the tourists.

At one point, they take a break at a tea house near the spot where Siddhartha Gautama was born. As legend has it, Gautama was born into wealth but gave it up to become a wandering ascetic. Later, he became known as the Buddha, "the Awakened One." Buddha followed the Vedas, which taught that the cause of human suffering is craving. Peace comes when you eliminate craving. Buddha went further. Through meditation, he showed how a person can achieve not just peace but a "transparent radiance of stilled mind" that can open into "transcendent knowing." The self dissipates into an "unsentimental embrace of all existence" where there are no longer any attachments to the past or the future. All that remains is mindful attention to the moment.[22]

I stopped reading. I wanted the narrator to take the next plane out of there so he could go see his son. I wanted him to face the loss of his wife head-on. I wanted him to look back at his life instead of walking, endlessly it seemed, into an unsentimental embrace of the present. I wanted the kind of story that the book would not tell.

A week later, I started reading again. I could see the analogy to prison now. The journey through the Himalayas is like the journey through prison. Both are full of discomfort and danger, deprivation and loss. Both challenge you to stay mindful in the moment, to seek out a transcendent kind of knowing, a freedom from the prison of the mind.

I stopped reading again. The analogy seemed off. Matthiessen could leave the mountain. A prisoner could not just leave the jail. But I could. Why, then, would I come back? What was I searching for?

* * *

"The fellas are fired up," John told me the next time we walked through the basement heading to school. "No one is teaching anything like this. No one is going personal."

"Really?"

"They get NA, God, GED. Sometimes a job program. That's about it."

"They get you."

"Ah, well," he demurred. "They are stuck with me, that's true." We spent the rest of the walk talking about the students, the ones with potential, the ones with heart, the ones that are easy to like no matter what, the ones that are not. He locked me in the classroom again, then returned minutes later with a battalion of writers. They took their seats quietly. A few said hello and thanked me for coming. Most sat in silence. They seemed unusually disciplined. When I heard the door close and saw John make his way across the room to his desk, I noticed some were watching him without watching him, sensing his movement and his mood. A few new faces had replaced those he kicked out for reasons that were not revealed to me.

I handed out copies of Pablo Neruda's poem "The Builder." It describes a man who chose an illusion that "divided up the dreams" of his life. Then he goes to the coast and sees "the beginnings of the ship." He touches it. It "quivered like the harp of heaven." Then the ship leaves and does not come back. Everyone who sees the ship leave cries, except the narrator, who goes "back to the wood with an ax," presumably to make a new ship. "My faith lay in those ships," he concludes. "I have no recourse but to live."[23]

We discussed the drama in the poem. Then I asked them to write about a false illusion that they once pursued. Fifteen minutes passed in swollen silence. Some wrote as if racing, hunched over their marbled composition books, elbows out. Others wrote sparingly, holding their page up for scrutiny, then putting it down to consider it again. Some finished early, closed their comp books, and waited. Others were still writing when I called time and asked for volunteers to read aloud. A slender man rose from his seat, put one arm behind his back—this seemed to be the ritual—and gripped his paper with the other.

"My name is Emanuel."

"HI EMANUEL!" the room boomed. Suddenly, it felt like an NA meeting. He smiled, revealing a few gold teeth, then began to read a poem about the illusion he pursued, becoming the dope man out on Broad Street. He gave us the backstory about his adolescent insecurities. The crooked teeth. The big feet. But the money he got from selling enabled him to get the jewelry and the clothes and the car and the respect of the players and, of course, the girls. He knew in retrospect that this was all about his low self-esteem. He knew what he had to do now to rebuild his life.

After class, John ordered the men to the hall, locked me in, and escorted them back upstairs to the tier. When he returned, he gathered his things, and we began the slow walk down the hall. As we went, he surprised me with a gift. A book by Jean Giono, *The Man Who Planted Trees*. The dust jacket was well-worn. It was an old copy. He started explaining it as I opened it up. Beautiful woodcuts illustrate the story of Elzéard Bouffier, who sets out planting trees in southern France before the First World War. Nobody asks him to do it. Nobody really knows he is doing it. He just keeps walking and making holes in the earth and dropping acorns into them. Three decades later, a forest appears.[24]

The next time I saw John, he let me know I could bring some students from campus. They would just need to do the background check, and that wouldn't take too long. So, I started to bring small groups of students from my prison literature class.

"Why not bring some other professors?" he asked a few weeks after that. "You could have more than one class at a time, you know." So, we made plans to do just that.

A year later, we created a college program, Open Minds, offering classes at the jail taught by VCU professors and taken by VCU students and residents at the jail. All the classes taught students how to dialogue respectfully and imaginatively about their shared humanity; to write creatively and analytically in search of common ground; and to link the liberal arts to personal experience. In addition to my writing class, we now had a gender studies class taught by Liz Canfield, a Zen Buddhism class taught by Jon Waybright, an African American literature class taught by Shermaine Jones, and a music studio run by Andy McGraw. It became a regular part of the semester, going to the jail with students from the university to have class with the students inside.

John planted the seed for this. But I was not as bold as Elzéard Bouffier. I could not grow the forest alone. I had to meet with the university lawyers. Naturally, there were concerns about safety, liability, publicity, and authority. It was not easy to merge the egalitarian environment of the university with the top-down, militaristic environment at the jail.

University officials were accustomed to seeing students as citizens and paying customers with rights. Jail officials were accustomed to seeing prisoners as lawbreakers who had forfeited their rights. They had no problem removing someone from a program if he acted up, and they assumed they would do the same with a VCU student. To avoid having a VCU student arbitrarily kicked out of a course for which they had already paid, I asked the staff to write down their rules. That way, we could prepare.

There were other disconnects between the culture of the university and the culture of jail. Public relations people at the university like to take pictures of the students and create stories to put on the website. They like to promote the brand. Their counterparts in jail don't readily share who is locked up in there. They like to promote the sheriff on their website. At first, I was told I would not be able to take any pictures of the prisoners in class for the Open Minds website. Later, I was permitted to take some, so long as the sheriff's staff could nix any they didn't like. I didn't mind. I wasn't worried about details like these. I *could* see the forest for the trees.

13

Not Many Fathers

Dave

Spring, 2011. Broad Street was already something of a party on my walk home from the university. The air was fragrant with cigarillos and marijuana. A guy was drinking beer from a can wrapped in a black plastic bag. A woman with spidery nails was showing her phone to a friend, who gasped dramatically. The street lights mixed with the music from the cars. Buses hissed and beeped at their stops. I heard him before I saw him. Dean's laugh was like a trombone skipping down the scale.

"Ha-ha! Dave! What's going on?" He wore a flat-rimmed Yankees cap, a blue starter jacket, and white kicks.

"Just heading home from class."

"Oh, all right, all right. Hey, Dave, this is Deonte." I stopped and set my backpack down. Deonte gave me a brief nod. "Dave's an English professor at VCU," Dean added. Deonte looked back and forth between Dean and me, not knowing what to make of the situation.

"We were just talking football, Dave. But I know you don't follow no sports. Ha-ha!"

"I play a little basketball when my kids are on the playground," I offered.

"Oh, you do, huh?"

"Just for the exercise."

Dean leaned over to Deonte, bumped his shoulder, then turned to me and leaned in.

"You got game, Dave?" he asked in a sly tone. Deonte's silence boiled over into an explosive giggle. He and Dean exchanged guttural quips that

I could not decipher but could tell, overall, were creating a story about the little white guy with game.

"Why don't you come hang out with me sometime at the Chimborazo courts to see for yourself?"

Deonte and Dean looked at each other at exactly the same time. "Oh no, he didn't!" Dean said.

"Oh yes, he did!" Deonte shot back. And then Dean was really laughing that melodious laugh of his, each note coming out lower than the last until the sound was so deep in his belly that it had nowhere else to go but up into the soft landing of his throat, into a breathy "ha-*haaa*!" that just went on and on. His elbow found my ribs.

Dean did come out to meet me at Chimborazo that weekend. He stood left of center court at the three-point line. I stood down court watching. He brought the ball back with his right hand, centered it with his left, cocked his head like he was looking through the scope of a rifle, and let it arc into an easy swoosh. I hustled after the ball and bounced it back. He made another three-pointer but missed the next. I took a turn, missed one, made one, and so on until we took a break to sit in the shade on the cement wall. A police car slowed to a stop on 29th Street adjacent to where we sat.

"Is that your ride?" I asked, only half joking.

"What?" Dean sputtered, indignant. "Nah!" But as he said it, he looked away, avoiding my eyes.

"Are you selling weed again?" I had no evidence. Nothing but my suspicion that he had been selling that night I saw him on Broad, probably to Deonte. I suspected that he was selling when he was not working at the steakhouse—that he was selling for the money but also for the camaraderie.

"Look," I said, lowering my voice. "I don't have any issue with you smoking weed. I just don't want to see you in jail again."

"Nah!" he kept saying until the silence took over. I can't remember how the visit ended.

Months later, I saw him in my office. He was frustrated. He was supposed to have a visit with his daughter the day before, but it got canceled. The real problem, he explained, was that he did not have custody. The baby's mama had given it to her mama. And Grandma did not always honor the court-mandated visits. He would show up at her house on the right day and time, only to find no one home. She would not answer the phone. She would not return his calls. He wanted to be a good father. But he felt trapped between that desire and the shape of his reality.

He found a picture of his daughter, Amaya, on his phone. He turned the screen to show me. "She's graduating from elementary school this year. I can't believe it!" He beamed.

"What school?"

"Oh, okay, okay. Hold on. Let me think." He leaned back in his chair, touching the side of his head.

Didn't he know where she went to school? Then I thought some more about it. If he'd lost custody, he may have been shut out from information like that. Plus, he didn't drive, so he probably didn't take her to school or pick her up like I did. And if he was getting shut out of court-mandated visits, maybe he was getting shut out of the day-to-day events at the school? I felt my chest tightening. I had never imagined an impediment to parenting.

"I know it's in Northside," he said.

"Is it Ginter?" I guessed.

"Nah, it starts with an H. Or maybe an L." I slapped the office desk like it was a buzzer and I was a contestant on *Wheel of Fortune*. I was ready to solve the puzzle.

"Linwood Holton Elementary School!"

"That's it!"

"My daughter goes there, too!"

"Get out of here!" Oh, how we high-fived. Maybe they knew each other? Maybe they were friends?

"What are you doing later this afternoon?"

"Nada."

"Why don't you take a ride with me to the school? Maybe you can see her at dismissal?" Grandma might be able to block him from those visits at her home, but she could not block me from bringing Dean to school at pickup just to say hi to his girl.

The lawn was packed. A white mom in Birkenstocks was sipping from a thermos. A Black mom in business casual was talking on her cell phone. A local politician in a suit was chatting with a thick-bearded man in paint-splattered boots. When the bell rang, the parents surged toward the door like it was the main stage at a concert. Kids spilled from the school in a splash of chatter and shrieks. Lucy ran full speed toward me, pivoting left, then right, outrunning her friends Madeline and Travis in a game of tag. Apparently, I was the base.

"Looks like you won!" Dean said to Lucy. She nodded, huffing, satisfied. I asked if she had seen Amaya in school today. She nodded, then watched me as I scanned the big lawn. I introduced Dean as Amaya's father. They smiled at each other.

"I don't usually see her after school, though," Lucy said. A line of buses pulled out from behind the school. The buses! I had forgotten about the kids who rode the bus. They get dismissed from the back of the school.

"You think she's on one of those buses?" I asked Dean. He shrugged.

"We used to call them the big yellow cheese," he told Lucy. She looked at the yellow bus rimmed in black with gaping windows like so many holes in a block of Swiss. She and Dean burst out laughing. Madeline and Travis laughed, too, then ran off to find their parents.

As Dean, Lucy, and I walked to my car, I remembered Dean's stories about his father not showing up for his football games and breaking whatever plans they had made. It crushed him. His father was more focused on running the streets, chasing women, and getting high. He'd missed the joy of parenting that Dean grasped intuitively.

The lifespan psychologist Erik Erikson has argued that parenting is a key way of becoming generative in middle age. Caring for a child is one way of moving beyond the earlier stages in which a person focuses primarily on the self. It is a way of giving back, passing on what you know, and watching life grow. That's how it's always been for me. Erikson concludes that, "Care is the widening concern for what has been generated by love, necessity, or accident; it overcomes the ambivalence adhering to irreversible obligation."[25] Dean had no ambivalence. He only wanted to fulfill his obligation.

* * *

I sat on a silver stool bolted to the ground, waiting for the visit to start. The glass in front of me was thick and scratched. The cinder block walls were light blue and jutted out a few feet to make a modest partition. This suggested privacy from other people visiting in their stalls but fell short of achieving it.

"Mr. Coogan!" I heard from somewhere below my line of vision. I turned around and looked down. A little boy was standing before me, wearing a big grin and a cap.

"Do I know you?"

He nodded with his whole body.

"How do I know you?"

"From school. From Lucy!" I was stumped.

"Take off your cap." He pulled it off.

"Oh, hey, Travis."

"Travis!" A woman's voice summoned him. "C'mon now, baby, your daddy's here." He put his cap back on and scurried toward the voice.

On the other side of the glass, Dean leaned against the cinder block wall and sighed. He picked up the black phone and brought it to his face. Slowly, I picked up mine. It was the first time we were seeing each other in this jail since we had the writing class in the chapel five years prior.

"You were right, Dave. You were totally right." I thought back to our conversation on the Chimborazo courts, just three months ago. I did not want to be right.

"I was trying to put a little something together to get over, you know? I need a bigger place with an extra bedroom for Amaya and her sister. I need a car to take her around."

Instantly, I thought about Lucy's room. I thought about my car. I thought about the material things that made it possible for me to be a father.

"You don't belong in here," I said. He nodded. *I know*. Slowly, he raised a fist up to the glass. Just as slowly, I offered mine.

* * *

"Mr. Coogan!" I heard as I walked through the halls of the school. I had just dropped off Lucy at her classroom and was heading out. Travis was heading in unaccompanied. We stood like reeds in the middle of the hall as a current of parents and kids flowed around us.

"Hey, Travis. Good to see you this weekend." I stopped myself from saying more. He fished for something to say.

"You were on the A side. I was on the B side," he offered, referring to the jail's two long, cinder block stalls for visitation.

"That's right," I said as I looked into his eyes. He turned away and sighed. I wondered if he was thinking of his dad. I wanted to ask if he'd had a good visit, but I didn't want anyone overhearing. I didn't know if anyone knew his dad was in jail.

When the second bell rang, his mood brightened. He walked away smiling, then turned back to shout goodbye. Although he was surrounded by people, he looked terribly alone. And I was suddenly sad. I had to get out of that hallway. I had to get back to my car. If I didn't, I would cry right there. Then someone would ask me what was wrong or try to comfort me, and I would have to lie. So, I steeled myself and waved back to Travis, wondering if his father had ever stood here and done the same thing.

Dean's return to jail did not last long. About six months. But he did lose the place where he was staying, and even some visits with Amaya. When he got out, he had to start all over again while living with his mother. He asked me to go with him to family court. He wanted to try to get more visitation hours. We sat in the courthouse lobby in vinyl chairs low to the ground.

"That's her," Dean said. He gestured to the far end of the lobby. I saw a tiny white woman with short, brown-grey hair, a tweed skirt, and a dark blazer. She had wiry energy and was, at this moment, talking to Amaya's grandma, who was seated and shaking her head over and over, dead set against whatever was being offered.

"The guardian ad litem. Her name is Penny," Dean informed me. Penny bustled toward us. When she was before us, Dean introduced me as a friend who had come to support. Penny nodded with enthusiasm and opened her leather binder.

"We have some barriers," she began. "For starters, there was the recent jail time. The judge will likely see that as a pattern of unreliability and possible risk to the child, exposing the girl to criminal activity."

"What? Name a case of mines where there was criminal activity in my crib!" She paged through her notes.

"That's right!" Dean continued. "There are none! And what about the last visits that she did not honor? Can we argue to get those back?" Penny conceded the possibility but noted that there were other barriers: his spotty record of paying child support, his lack of a car to take her places, including to the doctor if there was an emergency, and his small apartment without a second bedroom.

"I have a job now. I'll start paying again."

"And I have a car." I hadn't meant to say it; it just came out. I told Penny that I had driven them to the movies before and could do it again. I added that my daughter goes to the school where his daughter just graduated, near where Grandma lives.

"I am often in that neighborhood to pick up my daughter from school. I could drive Dean and Amaya back to my neighborhood for their visits. They could use the Chimborazo playground. I live right by there." Her blue eyes beamed.

"Did you say Chimborazo?"

"Yes."

"The one with the basketball courts," Dean interjected.

"Which house is yours?" Penny asked. When I described the yellow clapboards, the red barrel-shaped roof, and the gate we often forget to close, she marveled and marveled, until, at last, she revealed that she lived next door! When I shared that I was an English professor at VCU and that I met Dean as his writing teacher at the jail, she grew even more animated about the argument she could make in court.

"This is good. You are his mentor, a professor, and a father! You would provide a safe environment. You could supervise!" It made me cringe, hearing it narrated back this way. But it did not matter. When we got into court, and Penny made the case, the judge denied her request for more visitation hours.

"Your Honor," Dean began. "If Amaya can't come to my apartment, and she can't come to the playground with the professor and me, then when and where will she see me?" The judge leaned forward in his chair and straightened the papers in front of him.

"Mr. Turner, I understand that you are upset now. But you need to understand—"

"And when will she see her other grandmother, my mother?" He gestured back to the gallery where his mother sat. The people in the court, who were already quiet, got vacuum-sealed-container quiet. He had just interrupted the judge. And he was still going. "And when will she see her aunt?" He gestured to his sister, seated next to his mother. "Or the professor?" He pointed to me, sitting on his mother's other side. The judge's face, pale and slender, hardened into a point.

"Mr. Turner!" he snapped. Then he stood and turned his back on all of us.

"All rise," the deputy commanded. We rose. The judge left the courtroom without rendering a judgment. The deputies did not know what to do. We remained standing for several minutes in an awkward silence. When the judge reemerged a minute later, it was like he had just passed through a mood-altering machine.

"Please be seated," he said kindly. Slowly, we sat. "Mr. Turner, I want to commend you. Not many fathers come to this courtroom. And if they do, they do not come as you have today, seeking *more* time with their child. If they show up at all, it is to resolve a grievance about their responsibilities." That sounded right. That sounded like the opening to a concession for more time.

"Nevertheless, the visitation agreement that was arranged at the last court proceeding cannot be amended until you show more progress on self-sufficiency, consistent employment, adequate housing, child support payments, transportation, and the avoidance of incarceration."

I couldn't see Dean's face, but I could see him shaking his head in frustration. I felt it, too. It was the strangest conclusion. How could the judge recognize the good intentions of a father and then use his authority to block them?

* * *

The parents were pulling metal chairs from racks and setting them up in rows on the gymnasium floor. Lucy was somewhere in a swirl of kids that crested and foamed in a wave that eventually lapped over and into these seats. The hushing began when David Hudson, the principal, approached the podium in a stylish suit. He had the bearing and good looks of Marvin Gaye from the *What's Going On* album. Collar up, staring off toward the horizon of his purpose.

"Good evening, everyone," he said in a sonorous voice.

"Good evening, Mr. Hudson," the children intoned, pulling some parents into the ritual. Dean sat behind me with Amaya, her mother, and Grandma, who sat upright and unsmiling in a church dress. After the graduation ceremony, Dean introduced us.

She told me she was a piano teacher and began describing how she ran the lessons. I got a clear picture of a teacher whose kids probably feared if they did not practice, if they forgot their sheet music, if they touched her piano with dirty hands, if they said something wayward, intentionally or not, if they were anything less than respectful and prepared and perfect. I received her credentials with a small nod, affirming her authority as a teacher, which seemed to be her aim. Then she told Amaya that it was time to go.

14
The Script

Dave

Fall, 2012. G flopped hard on the little office chair and let out a flat tire of a sigh. He shook his head and stared out the window. Eventually, he told me why he was there. His baby mama's house got shot up last night.

I had not met the baby mama he'd written about in jail, but I was now meeting the baby, a sturdy girl, maybe four or five years old, in a brown dress. She seemed unsure where she was or who I was. G did not explain. I gave her my desk chair and some paper and pens. She began drawing without talking, angling her face close to the paper in a mask of concentration or fear. I could not tell which.

"Why did they shoot up the house?" I heard myself asking, quietly, casually, like I was accustomed to asking this kind of question, like G was just another student come to talk about a paper.

G snorted. "Hey, I stuck to the script," he began. But the other guys did not. Apparently, he and some acquaintances had driven up Interstate 95 to New Jersey to get a pack of crack. The trouble started when they got back to Richmond. Instead of waiting to meet their connect, the other guys started selling the drugs that night. They either didn't know or didn't care that they were selling on another guy's block. I couldn't believe what I was hearing. The whole point of the class at the jail was to write your way out of scenes like this.

"Do you like to gamble?" I asked G, following his gaze out the window.

"What?" He winced like I hadn't heard a word he'd said. Then he warmed up to the topic. "Yeah, I'll go online sometimes. Play poker."

"Do you like to gamble with life?"

He groaned. "You don't get it."

"I think I do. When you got off 95 and drove back to your girl's mother's house with those drugs, you were gambling. The wager was their lives." He shook his head, growled, then pushed up from the chair, sliding it back into the bookcase. The little girl got up and reached for his hand, but G was already halfway out the door. She rushed to catch up, abandoning her unfinished drawing on my desk. A house with two windows, a front door, shrubs, and a street leading nowhere.

When I told a friend the story of G's drug run up 95, she listened intensely, nodding and nodding like she had already heard it, until her voice took over.

"It's like *The Wire*!" she exclaimed. I hadn't seen it. She insisted I watch it, especially the episodes involving D'Angelo Barksdale.

Once a promising dealer in his uncle Avon's drug empire, D'Angelo loses favor when he shoots and kills a rival dealer in front of a witness. The police investigate. The case goes to court. Avon berates D'Angelo for making the whole operation a target, then sends him up I-95 to New Jersey to bring drugs back to Baltimore. It's a setup. Avon pulls some strings to get him arrested and sent to prison. Like a pawn in a game of chess, D'Angelo is sacrificed to do the king's bidding.

This is where the analogy to the show broke down. G was not a pawn. His story was not prefigured by scriptwriters trying to maximize drama. He was alone in his narrative.

G brought his girlfriend to my office one day unannounced, much like he brought his daughter. And like his daughter, she seemed uncertain why she was there. She looked like someone taking a break from an office job. Big boned in a light blouse with dark slacks. A shadow of uncertainty crossed her face as G explained that he had gotten a probation violation and wanted us to be his character witnesses. He thought we should meet before court. It seemed like this was the first time she was hearing about his background, and she was now having second thoughts about the relationship. After she left to get back to work, I asked G how he'd met her. He grinned like a little boy holding in a secret.

"Okay," he said at last. "I'll tell you." He stretched his legs out wide and smiled. "I was out on Broad with my boy, Shawn, you know, just chilling. And he pointed her out. He was like, 'Yo, that's where the money's at!'" G lingered there at the memory of that day. "For real? I was going to rob her. But I changed my mind after I started talking to her."

I tried to imagine the woman who had just left my office walking alone down the sidewalk as two men discussed attacking her, stealing her purse. I felt something acidic creeping up my throat. I swallowed hard to make it go away. He noticed my discomfort.

"I know, right? It's crazy!" He laughed. I shook my head side to side and reached for a pack of gum.

The next time I saw G was in court. The girlfriend and I stood on his left side. His lawyer stood to the right. After the judge finished lecturing G, he asked him who we were. My knees began buckling, undermining my resolve, as I heard G identify me as "Dr. David Coogan from VCU." The judge and his deputies looked up, intrigued. I felt like a shopper who had been standing in the walk-in beer cooler too long—wishing for warmth, willing to leave without selecting anything. I said something. The girlfriend said something. G got no jail time, just another fine. As we turned to leave, I heard the judge warning G to listen to the counsel of the good people he had brought to court today. I walked out as fast as I could without drawing attention to myself.

It began to feel like G was using my office like a break room in the job of his life, a place he could go to complain, recharge, or brainstorm his next move. Sometime after that court date, G brought his mother by unannounced. Her face was flat and round like his. She had dark bags under her eyes. He did not give her my name. He did not really introduce us except to say *this is my mother* and *this is the professor*. She acknowledged me briefly, glanced at my diplomas, then fixated on the carpet.

"This is the man making the book," G explained. "I'm putting my story in there." Then he moved his chair closer and found her ear. "I'm going to put everything in there," he threatened. "Everything!" She covered her face. I wanted to disappear.

He opened a notebook he'd brought with him and began to read a piece about growing up in the housing projects in New York City. She was out getting high. Some nights she would not come home, and he would wander the building. Eventually, he got out into the streets. He was big for his age and soon learned how to hold his own in a fight. He began robbing people, robbing stores, and sleeping on the train. He was ten years old. It was a blister of a story. He kept probing the tender parts. Her shoulders began to heave.

"The problem with drugs for a little kid," he concluded, "is that the drugs get all the attention!" When at last he finished irritating the memories, she lifted her head and looked at me. Her eyes were wet. G was glaring at her, breathing heavy through his nose.

"I know I am getting back now what I put in as a mother. I know that." I did not know that. I was not even thinking that. I was still squirming in the role that G had cast me in: The man from the university making the book, sitting here in judgment, the arbiter of their history. It was a role I had never imagined and certainly did not want. I had wanted to read about their mothers; I'd never imagined meeting those women, or seeing those writings used to shame them.

G stopped coming to the office after that. I could not get him on the phone. A few months later, a call came in on a number that I did not recognize. He was in Louisville. He needed money for the bus fare to get back to Richmond. He would not tell me why he was in Louisville. He danced around the question like a magician, making it disappear. Kelvin later told me that Louisville was well-known by guys in Richmond as a good place to get clean and sober. They had some good programs. I assumed that's why G had gone.

G wanted the money sent via Western Union. He promised he would pay me back. I was wary that lending money would alter the basis of our relationship, rooted in the class at the jail and the book project. Then I did a little work persuading myself. I reasoned that if he had gone to get sober and now wanted to come home, I would know when I saw him. If he was acting more humbly and wasn't getting in trouble, he was probably sober—or sober enough that he wouldn't be likely to commit crimes that could send him back to prison. If he took the money but came back wild and unreliable again, or did not come back at all, I would also have my answer. I reasoned that sending him the money would help me understand what was happening.

My only hitch was that I did not want to send the money through Western Union. I had never used the service and was suspicious when I saw the steep fees. I told him I would send a real check. Reluctantly, he agreed. A few days later, he called back to tell me he never got the check and that I needed to send it again to another address. He had moved. He wouldn't say why he'd moved. He wouldn't say why the post office could not forward mail from the old address. I still didn't know why he was in Louisville. At this point, I was done trying to figure out the story. I canceled the check and never sent another.

When at last he returned to Richmond several months later, he came to see me in the office. He did not talk about the check or about Louisville or about how he got back. He wanted to know when the book was going to be published. I showed him the rejection letters and emails from literary agents and publishers. I assured him this was all part of the process, that I was doing everything I could, that it just took time to get a book published. He felt he should already be making money from his writing; he had been out of prison for a few years now and had not seen any profit. When I pointed out that there could be no profit without a book to sell, he said he wanted out. When I explained that the only thing he was getting out of was a chance to help someone with his story and, down the road, a chance to get a small royalty check, he shook his head. His mind was made up. When I reminded him that he had signed an agreement to publish his story, he exploded.

"Write me a new agreement then!" I reached for a comp book, opened it, and began writing.

I, Dave, will take G's story out of the book that I am editing. I signed the page, tore it out, and gave it to him. Then I started a new page.

I, G, will not ask to have my story put back into the book that Dave is editing. He signed it. He left without saying goodbye.

Dean called a week later. He and G had bonded in the class and during reentry as fellow New Yorkers down here in the South. He told me he knew that G had pulled out of the book. He just wanted me to know G was doing okay. Dean had gotten him a job washing dishes at the restaurant where he was a cook. He was proud of that. And I was glad to hear it.

Dean called back the next day in a much different mood. G never showed up for work. Dean found out from mutual friends what happened. G had gone to a club the night before. He met a girl. They left the club together. On their way out, two other guys asked for a ride. The woman agreed. She had a Chrysler 300. A few minutes into the ride, one of the dudes in the back seat pulled a gun on them. The woman braked hard, jumped out, and ran. The dude shot G as he tried to get out of the car. He died there on the side of the road.

The crime report gave the location. It was not far from my house, not far from where Andre had died—a winding, tree-lined road with sudden hills that takes you out of the city. G died at a sharp curve where there is a street sign, but strangely no street to turn down. I imagined there probably was one before they put in the train tracks overhead and tore up the road. But who knows, really?

I pulled over, parked, and stood in the sandy half circle near the street sign. Sunlight pierced the leaves overhead. Grit scraped underfoot. I imagined the abandoned car, its doors gaping like hungry mouths, and G's big body slumped over the seats. I remembered his daughter's picture in my office. A house with two windows, a front door, shrubs, and a street leading nowhere.

15

Faith and Resilience

Ronald

In the fall of 2011, I began to date RG. He was right out of a dream. We met online and spent time talking on the phone. I had a picture of him. Then the day came when we were finally able to meet face-to-face.

I want everything to be perfect. I spend time on my hygiene, getting every piece of me just right. My head needs to be shaved perfectly smooth. My scent needs to be seductive. My outfit needs to be on point, every color matching. My underwear needs to be tight and right. My shoes need to be clean and the right colors.

I believe I'm ready. I can move out. I can show up and be on time. Prayer. I get on the bus headed to the subway, which I'll take to Johns Hopkins station, where RG is going to meet me in his car. Before I go down into the metro station, I text to let him know that I am on my way. He texts that he is on his way. I get to my stop, go up the escalator toward the street. Then I see him in his car. He cracks the window. And my heart melts. He is the breath of fresh air that I have been longing for. We fall in love instantly.

We were living identical lives—both living with exes, both rebuilding our lives following adverse childhood experiences that had lasted into adulthood. The more we bonded, the tighter we became. I would spend the days in his car, looking for work, and nights with him.

RG was twelve years older than me. He drank and smoked marijuana, but he was managing things well. We'd go out to the bar on weekends with our network of close friends. We didn't match in every area of our lives, but for the most part, we were a solid fit. RG was a big flirt and could attract anyone; however, he played the innocent role of not knowing they were flirting with him. Through our talks, we decided to invite compatible people into a sexual relationship that had boundaries. One of them was not kissing. Kissing can lead to attachment.

RG let me use his car while he was at work. This allowed me to get a job with Burger King, so I was now able to contribute to the relationship financially. Through my effort, RG was able to see that I was an equal partner. But there were flaws. When he found out that I did not have my driver's license, he began to urge me to be cautious.

At this time, I was living with my former lover, Anthony, and his current lover. Anthony's insecurities about his lover and me having a friendship brought tension. He had instructed his lover to deny me the privilege of using the internet. One day, Anthony came home from work early and found me using the internet. He proceeded to hit his lover. He knocked him to the ground and began to really beat on him. Then he turned to me.

We threw punches at each other. Anthony then grabbed a kitchen knife and began to chase me and his lover, who ran out the door. I ran upstairs while calling 911. When the Baltimore City Police showed up, they politely listened to our story. But the result was that all three of us were arrested and hauled to the lockup. This caused me to go into a fury. Are you going to punish me as well? I was the one who called 911 because I was afraid! Now you're just going to send us to lockup to let the courts iron it out? I had already endured too much abuse, mistrust, and injustice at the hands of our government systems. How was this justice? RG came and bailed me out of jail. But once again, I found myself homeless.

The situation was out of my control. After years of changing and working to restore my life and be productive in society, I had again found myself within the confines of this country's alleged justice system. As the days passed, the anger I felt at being arrested traumatized me all over again. After being bailed out, I continued to be as productive as possible. I went to work and filled my spirit with the joy of the customers. Working in fast food and training to become a certified peer recovery coach, I tried to find my purpose. I became more determined to grow spiritually, to be at peace, to know joy, and to be a loving individual. For the next few years, I would spread the message of transformative justice, as opposed to reforming the criminal justice system. Most people don't understand that reforming the system is just tinkering within an unjust system. Nothing changes when everything remains the same. There's no compassion. No help. The system just traumatizes you in another way. *Transforming* the system starts with changing the people, policies, and procedures. It's a fresh start with diversity, equity, and inclusion. Everyone matters.

Within our first year together, RG and I got a place together and learned a lot about each other. Then something changed. RG started denying me sex. I had seen this pattern before, with Anthony and others. But whereas before, I would resort to cheating, I decided to try something different this time and work on our compatibility. RG still desired a sexual outlet, so we engaged in threesomes. But I began to notice his heart had hardened toward me. I tried everything I could think of, but it didn't bring him back to me. Six months after moving into our new place, we separated and became roommates.

It took me six more months to become better with me. I did not yet know that I was resilient. And I had to live with someone who I was still in love with but who was treating me like I was invisible. I endured emotional and mental abuse from RG every day as I struggled to keep it together. I was building up my resume and progressing as best I could, learning to be better to myself. My self-confidence began to grow. I grew spiritually and matured. I was healing from those traumatic wounds of the past. Despite the naysayers and haters, I was still recovering.

I was fired from Burger King in August of 2013. The store manager felt like I was insubordinate. But I was just speaking up for myself; I had too much self-respect. When she came to grab my headset, I thought she was coming to hit me. She told me I was fired. So, I cussed her.

After that, I managed to get a job at a McDonald's in Dundalk, a majority-white neighborhood, where I endured racism and biased treatment as an employee. I was a manager-in-training. One of the managers I worked with was a woman who talked to the other employees in a pleasant voice. But with me she used a stubborn, put-down voice. Nothing I could do was right. One time, she snatched a cup out of my hands and threw it in the trash. Then she dropped my schedule down to two days a week.

Eventually, I completed my peer recovery coach course trainings; however, my certification was delayed, as one of the conditions was maintaining consistent employment. I needed to find a better job with more hours. But I couldn't just quit McDonald's. So, I forced myself to stay.

In January of 2014, I went to work at a Wawa in Dundalk, a convenience store that offered good benefits. However, once again, I endured racism. Dundalk was just not a community used to dealing with Black people.

Talking with my mom, who was still in Richmond battling health problems, I covered for the abuse I was suffering. The Wawa manager treated me indifferently, as the McDonald's manager had done, reducing me to two days a week. But I believe in the unseen. I know that I need to talk it, walk it, and live it, without getting to see the joy in it. Despite the emotional turmoil I was going through, God showed up and showed out with blessings all the way.

I wrote the manager a letter asking why my hours were cut. She called me into the office. She told me she had a business to run and didn't have time to read letters. I told her that if I were to remain a store associate, I needed more hours. I cried out. Two weeks later, I was moved back to forty hours a week and was on track to be considered for a manager position.

Good news finally came from Professor Coogan in the beginning of that year: He had found a publisher for our book, which I had basically given up hope on. It had been nearly four years since we'd stopped writing. I rejoiced for him in his diligent promotion of the book. I was seeing sunnier skies.

I interviewed for a second job as a porter at a grocery store that was going to be opened in Rosedale. They liked me and hired me as shift manager instead. Wow, now I was blessed with two full-time jobs. My income increased a lot. I was grateful and beginning to believe that the impossible was possible, and anything I attempted, I could accomplish. I had recently rededicated my life to my Lord and Savior at the Greater Gethsemane Missionary Baptist Church. My faith was deepening, and I was learning to have a relationship with God that had substance. I was transforming.

In trusting God, I was learning to let go and let God. I applied to Walmart. It took me eight months to get through that door, but I made it in. When filling out the application, I finally faced my past by straight-up listing as many of my convictions as I could remember. I am a three-time convicted felon in the state of Virginia. But those convictions are over twenty years old. I was the first felon that store had ever employed, which meant I had something to prove.

In May of 2015, I resigned from Wawa and the grocery store and began my journey at Walmart as their claims associate. My manager was in the Maryland National Guard. He was really relaxed in the job. As he was training me, he got into a dispute with one of the floor managers, and after three days, I found myself in the job alone. Learning the job on my own was tough. I was responsible for processing damaged, misused, and returned products and filing insurance claims for the company to get reimbursement. I was also responsible for hazardous waste to keep us in compliance with local, state, and federal laws, as well as OSHA.

Quarterly, we would receive a bonus if we made our quotas. I decided that as soon as I was eligible, I was going to earn that bonus. After I made that goal, I received three more bonuses during my time with Walmart. I made it a point to be kind to people. There was this one lady who came to work and never spoke to anyone. I always smiled and talked to her. Eventually, she began to smile and speak to me. I could tell it was Sir Ron who had shown up. I helped bring a new spirit to a place where there was a black cloud hanging.

As you read my story, please don't have sympathy for me. The corners and curves I have faced in life have led to my confidence. These were the fires that built my faith, the tribulations that gave me my testimony. My trials have made me triumphant. I am a spiritual being with my humanity intact. I am Black, bisexual, and in long-term recovery from incarceration and substance use. I have mental health diagnoses of bipolar disorder and post-traumatic stress disorder. I live with an illness, HIV, that wants my life daily. Significantly, I am blessed by God with pain, and I will find purpose. My trauma will be healed.

Facing these hardships has given me the courage to find my voice and use it to speak for the voiceless. It has given me the strength to withstand the pain and get to the peace, love, and joy of the moment. My organization, LIVE, has been built through me for God. Everything that threatened my demise became a great resource for my rise.

My attitude of gratitude comes from my heavenly Father and supports my relationship with all things. My Father forgave my mistakes so that I may have another chance. Feeling failure enabled me to see there is no failure in God. He will use all of me to get glory from my story.

16
Meet the Author

Dave

Winter, 2015. The air was crisp. The sun was gone. Stan leaned against the side of the building. He wore a charcoal suit with a white pocket square and a soft blue shirt open at the neck. He just got out of prison a month ago, but it looks like he just got out of a glossy magazine photo shoot. He lowered his cigarette and let out a stream of blue smoke as I approached.

"Looking good, Stan."

"They say you should dress how you feel." He flicked ash from the cigarette.

"And how do you feel?"

"Important, Dave. This is an important night." He winked like a leading man in an old movie. He took another pull off the cigarette, dropped it on the sidewalk, and crushed it underfoot.

"Let's do this, Coogan."

I nodded and opened the door of the Black Iris Gallery. It was packed. Some people were leaning against the walls. Others were sitting in white folding chairs set up in rows. There were people from my neighborhood. People from the church. People from the university. People from nonprofits that I had worked with in the city. People I did not know, but who I could tell were connected to the guys just by the way they were watching them or bantering with them. The mood was elevated, with overlapping conversations and sudden shots of laughter. My family was in the back with the boxes of books. After years of searching the country for a publisher, I'd ultimately found one right here in Richmond. And by that time, I had figured out how to tell my story of teaching the guys to write their stories. When I sent my manuscript to Brandylane Publishers, it was finally a book ready to be published.

Stan and I made our way to the stage to join the guys. Terence was in a yellow button-down shirt and a dark tie. He was quiet and watchful, as I suspected he would be before such a big crowd. Dean sat back with his legs stretched out, running a hand through his fresh, short haircut. Kelvin wore all black, which did nothing to tamp down his good mood. He was already laughing at something Dean just said. Naji had on a flowing white sweater that offset his rich, ebony skin. His partner, Cassandra, sat in the front row, beaming. Stan took the seat next to me and draped one arm over the back of my chair. A gold watch dangled loosely from his wrist. His sister Shelia sat in the middle of the audience, smiling big enough for the whole room to see.

Beads of sweat dotted Naji's brow. He chewed gum with the ferocity of a boxer adjusting a mouth guard. The chewing and power baldness gave him a masculine intensity.

"I can't stop sweating," he whispered to me. "And my heart is beating fast!"

"You'll be fine once we start," I assured him. He nodded.

I drifted in and out of the host's introduction. Then I heard my name. The audience began clapping. Someone gave me the mic. I told the story of how we came together nine and a half years ago at the jail. I praised the men for sticking with the class when they went to prison. I praised them for doing the hardest thing you can do in prison. Opening up. Digging through the past. Holding up the relics of experience to the light. Trying to piece the shards together into a story.

"They say nothing much ever comes out of prison . . ." I held up a copy of *Writing Our Way Out*, with our names on the front. "But this book happened!" The applause lapped over the stage. When it receded, I introduced the men one by one, leaving enough time for more applause after each name.

I gave Naji the mic. He pulled down the gold glasses from the top of his head and angled the mic so that he could see the book in his lap. Then he began reading a story about how and why he used to burglarize homes and businesses at night. His voice was deep with little trace of the nerves he'd described a moment before. He told the crowd he especially liked targeting homes in white neighborhoods where the curtains were drawn back, displaying the intimacy of the dwelling, as if the people living there had nothing to hide.

He knew that what he was doing was wrong. Behind the fierce imagery and precise diction was a reproving voice. The source of his anger was deep and complex. He remembered his childhood dreams deflating under the abuse he was experiencing at home. He remembered his core self dying with no one tending it. He remembered seeking deliverance from the put-downs he heard about his skin color. He remembered the boy who grew into the man who felt most alive at night, when he could disappear into the anonymity and possibility of becoming what he called the Black Ghost.

That man is traumatized, unfinished, alive. The author had taken a version of that man and made him a character in this story. In it, the character smashes a window and moves through it undetected. He is aware of the insanity of his actions. He knows the adrenaline rush is temporary. But he cannot stop. Naji read aloud from the book: "I live for the transformation, the freedom of becoming, without doubt or contradiction. The repercussions will leave a bitter taste in my mouth if I'm discovered, but I gladly risk it to be alive in this moment, knowing who and what I am." He looked up, stunned. He was done. The people were applauding intensely. Then they were standing. He was finally smiling.

It took some time for the applause to die down. When it did, I passed the microphone to Stan. He stood and thanked everyone for coming. Then he began reading his story about lifting weights in prison with guys like him who were more interested in sculpting their bodies than feeding their minds. Everyone laughed when he said was a member of the dumb dudes club filled with guys with "bulging biceps and legs like tree trunks and minds like babies." Then he asked readers to look again at the image and try to see beyond the stereotype—to look beyond the razor wire fences, the guards, and the guns. Look closer, he commanded, and "you'll see the chains. You'll see despair, hopelessness, and gloom. You'll see things that chain me to childhood. You'll see the wounds that have been festering for years. You'll see the prison inside me."

The story had ended. But Stan was just getting started. He had a faraway look in his eyes, eyebrows down, thoughts forming. He waited for people to finish clapping, holding the mic loosely below his chin. Then he sat down, lowered the book, and reclined.

"Can I just really talk to you?" he asked the audience. They let free a consoling sigh. Kelvin stifled a huge laugh, bending over to hide his face. Dean held his arm up and rolled his fist in a circle by his ear. *Keep going!*

"Look, I did twenty years. And it's a trip, right, because I'm uncomfortable *here*." He stood again, squared his shoulders, and raised his voice. "I'm uncomfortable here! But if *that guy* had a rape case . . ." He pointed to an imaginary guy somewhere in the audience and continued pointing as he spoke. "Or if *he* had a murder charge. Or if *he* killed that person. Or if *he* broke into that, or stole that, or got high off of everything he had . . . I was *comfortable* around that!" He pivoted quickly into a whisper. "I was comfortable, because their dysfunction was no different from my dysfunction!"

The literary critic Paul Eakin has described memoir as a genre dependent on an illusion of self-determination. The autobiographer is well aware that he is making a story. He is aware of selecting and shaping memories. But at the same time, he needs to believe that he is also finding a story already written—that he is showing us a self already formed. The illusion is that the writer can track the evolution of a "continuous identity" from then to now. What the writer really discovers is not a found identity, but "a kind of awareness in process"[26] of a changing self.

Stan scanned the room slowly. Nobody moved. Nobody spoke. It felt like minutes passing, but it was only a few seconds. Still, it was long enough to see the gap that had opened up between the author and the man. The author who wrote the piece in prison wanted people to really see him. Face-to-face with the audience he had once only imagined, he wasn't so sure he wanted to be seen, his mistakes and truths laid bare for people who might not understand. He lowered the mic, sat down, and leaned back in his chair, breaking the spell with a grin. The crowd erupted in applause. The man had just met the author.

17

Blessed

Kelvin

When I got home, I worked for a mason. I did construction. I was basically a laborer. I didn't mind. It wasn't nothing new. I always had a regular job, even back in the day when I was selling drugs. What's the alternative to working? I'm not a lazy guy. I wasn't one for sitting around doing nothing.

Now, these jobs I had weren't the best-paying jobs. So, I told Dave about it, and he asked if he could put it out there on Facebook. He put me out there in front of the whole world, asking for a job. If it wasn't Dave, I wouldn't have okayed it, even though I appreciated it. I still don't think I okayed the picture of me that he used, though. That was the worst part. He put a picture of me up on Facebook that made me look like a space alien! Like I was a greased-up Marvin the Martian. I hated the way it happened. But that's the way I got a job with Main Street Realty.

I went in as a porter. Doing maintenance work, fixing washers and dryers, replacing panels, electronic boards, going up on the roof. I was working under a guy named Daryl. I did all of his work. He got paid for it. That's how that went. He didn't want to do nothing. So, he put all his work on me. He was the worst supervisor.

Then I got put in with Mike and Jessie. Jessie was the exact opposite of Daryl. A real maintenance man. A young guy with an old man's mentality. Very experienced. I learned a lot from him. I ended up working on three buildings down in Shockoe Bottom. I was making $11.50 an hour. Then I got a fifty-cent raise. They couldn't pay me more until I went to school to get certified. After I did, I got $15.00.

There were times when I looked back on the old days and realized that selling drugs was some of the easiest money I ever made. I wished I could make it that easy again. Selling drugs is a very lucrative business if you don't get caught. But I did not want to get caught again. Doing that time changed me. My mind got turned around. I can't say I shook off the dope man mentality. But I shook off the lifestyle. I couldn't be that same person forever. Nobody can be the same person forever. To be truthful, it was basically fear. The fear of being locked away and not being able to do what I want to do. Putting my family through all that. That's the foundation of doing away with all that negative shit.

It's been years now since I've sold. What I did was switch my focus to another business. That way, I could still be a people person, just without drugs. I had a good idea how to do that. It wasn't no food truck. It was Fire and Ice—hot drinks in the winter, cold drinks in the summer. I actually started that business back in 2002, before going to prison. When I got home, I decided I needed to revive it. So, when Dave told me about the program with UnBoundRVA, I signed up. At the time, I felt that was the exact right place for me. It was a free class on how to set up and manage your business, designed for people like me who had done time or who needed more support in getting investors.

The best part of the class was sitting in a room full of people who were trying to do what I was trying to do, start their own business, their own brand. It was a nice experience in the beginning. But I didn't understand that it was set up as a competition: Best idea gets the bank loan, pro bono legal advice, and ongoing mentoring. And only one person gets it. I didn't like competing with others who were trying to achieve their dreams. I didn't understand why they set it up like that. If you have a group of us that needs help, why do we have to compete? That was the worst part. I didn't like the way it ended, with them choosing not to invest in my business and me getting no support from them moving forward. And I didn't like that Dave had to get involved, asking these people what I did wrong. I could see that upset him.

I had hit a rough patch. My car had broken down, and I couldn't get anything for it. I was homeless. But I was working. The next car I got came through Dave's friend Bob Patterson at St. Paul's. A Volvo S60 T6 Turbo. I couldn't believe he would give me a vehicle like that, just because Dave told the people in that church about my situation. Thinking about it now, that's been one of the best things that's happened to me since coming home, being blessed with transportation. That Volvo got me through a whole lot. I was able to keep my job at Main Street Realty, which had me going down to Southside and back to Shockoe Bottom to work in different buildings. I needed a car for that, because the bus was terrible.

That Volvo was a major building block in my reentry. I was able to get back and forth to see my grandkids. It was also my dog Dallas's favorite car. When I saved up to get a new vehicle, I decided instead of maintaining two, I would give the Volvo to Stan. I've always believed that if somebody does me a blessing, I should do the same. That way, somebody else could be blessed.

18

Dominion

Dave

Spring, 2016. Late morning light poured through the bay windows. The men wore suits or country club khakis. The women wore dresses, or skirts and blouses. Some balanced small cups of coffee on saucers. They were smiling, flush from a good service and ready for the program to begin. This morning, Kelvin, Brad, Terence, Stan, and I were the program in the gathering space at First Baptist Church.

The host offered a nice introduction, welcomed us, and then handed me the mic. After a few remarks about how and why I started the writing class at the jail, I announced that each man would read from his story. It got quiet as a theater when the lights dim as the program began.

Kelvin read a story about becoming a drug dealer in middle school. Brad read a piece about getting robbed at gunpoint by drug dealers when he couldn't pay off a cocaine bender. Terence shared the story of losing everything—his ROTC scholarship at VCU, his GPA, his marriage, his money—to his crack addiction. And Stan read the piece he'd read at the Black Iris, about the prison inside of him that chained him to childhood and despair. After he finished, we made our descent onto the tarmac of the Q & A.

A man in the front row raised his hand. His beard was blond-grey. He had a bolo tie. His face was pink like steak medium-well, and like steak it glistened. He scanned our faces from left to right, addressing each of us with clear, blue eyes.

"I want to know . . ." he paused as he shifted in his seat. "I want to know when each one of you first met Jesus and accepted him as your personal Lord and Savior." Brad caught my eye, patted his chest, and nodded. With his blond crew cut, Dockers, and plaid, button-down shirt tucked in with a belt, he could be a member of this church.

"I can tell you exactly when that was for me," he began. Leaves fluttered in the courtyard beyond the bay windows. A long line of sunlight stretched from the windows into the center of the room, revealing small swirls of dust.

"When I hit rock bottom, I was fed up with myself. I had the disease of addiction, but I didn't know it. It was all-consuming. All that time spent getting the money to get the drugs. It was exhausting. I don't know if any of you have been through it or known anyone who has, but it is a very selfish disease." Several heads bobbed with deep understanding. He continued.

"So, I was on the streets in DC. Homeless. Panhandling. And I realized I just couldn't do it anymore. I couldn't remember the last time I chose food over drugs. That's when I called a friend of mine to come get me and take me to the police. I turned myself in. I think I'm the only one in the book who did that. Is that right, Dr. Coogan?" I confirmed that it was right.

"In prison, I dried up. And when I dried up, I could think straight. It was maybe a few weeks later that it happened. I literally got down on my knees and began praying."

His voice had become like a cello. Notes unadorned, alone. Sweet and solid from the center of his chest. "I was born again that evening: June 20, 2004, 9:25 p.m." He stopped here at the crescendo of his story, looked away, and sighed.

An older woman sitting up front was overcome with longing. She reached over to grab the arm of her friend, dabbing her eyes with a tissue. A man in the middle of the room stood to applaud. That started it. Soon, husbands and wives, parents and children, seniors and single people, clergy and ushers followed suit. A standing ovation!

When they sat back down, Stan reached for the mic. Brad passed it to me, and I passed it to Stan, who stood, unbuttoned his suit jacket, tilted his head to the left, cracked a joint in his neck, and centered it again. He began pacing the stage, mic cord snaking around him like a tail. When he reached center stage, he planted his feet, faced the people, and held up an index finger.

"Okay, Genesis. Book of Genesis."

"Yes!" they respond.

"In the beginning, God created the earth. And when He was done, He gave dominion to who?" Cued this way, of course, the people knew the answer.

"That's right! Man! He gave it to Man. But you have to remember how *we* came here." He gestured to himself, Kelvin, and Terence. His voice dropped into a private confidence. "We didn't come as men. We were property. Chattel." He approached the man in the bolo tie. "Would you give dominion of the earth to your dog?"

The room began realigning. Some were murmuring and nodding. Others seemed to need more time. It was my first visit to First Baptist. I did not know if they were accustomed to thinking about race in the context of their faith. I later learned that questions about race were, in fact, a part of their history.

In the 1960s, the pastor of Richmond's First Baptist Church, Theodore Adams, supported the Civil Rights campaign to integrate the Southern Baptist Convention with the American Baptist Convention. This would have meant integrating Baptist churches in the south, many of them in rural communities, with large, Black churches in the cities. Adams, who was running for president of the Southern Baptist Convention, argued at that meeting that our "thunderous silence in the face of oppressive injustice for American Negroes has amounted to a serious complicity in the problem."

Not everyone agreed. R. W. Nevins, "a retired 90-year-old minister from Lexington, KY," counterargued that "forced integration by the federal government was unscriptural and an invasion of the sanctity of the home." Nevins went on to claim that "God made the white man white, and He wants him to stay white. He made the black man black, and He wants him to stay black. The devil made the mulatto." Adams lost the presidency to the segregationists.[27]

Nevins's racism is not actually in the Bible, of course. According to Charles Marsh, the Baptist justification for slavery came from an interpretation of the Bible story where Ham sees his father, Noah, drunk and naked one night. He tells his brothers, Shem and Japheth, who then cover their father with a blanket. When Noah finds out about it the next day, he becomes enraged and declares that Ham and his progeny would forever be servants to his brothers and their progeny.

Ham, Shem, and Japheth were all brothers living in a time before the concept of race had been invented. The Bible never specifies their skin color or the skin color of their descendants. Those interpretations would come later, when they were needed to provide scriptural support for the subjugation of Black people. Marsh explains that "by the early 1900s, many Southern Baptists had come to read the story as a convincing account of the origin of the black race, condemned to a legacy of servitude." [28]

The man in the front row conceded Stan's point about dominion. "I can see where you're coming from."

"But look, I don't say that to divide us. We've all just had different journeys," Stan elaborated. "You may have come down Cary and turned up Belvidere to get here," he pointed to the man with the bolo tie, conjuring a picture of his commute from Richmond's affluent West End. "But maybe I took 95? You know what I mean? We've all been on different paths in life. And sometimes we get lost."

"Yes," someone said.

"We do," another added.

"Brad was speaking about when he was lost up in the streets of DC, right? Well, I was lost, too, once. And I needed a guide."

"Preach!" Kelvin shouted.

"When the Israelites were fleeing the Egyptians, they needed a guide."

"Yes!" the people said. This was a song they knew.

"And who did they follow?"

"Moses!" the people exclaimed. "Moses!"

"Right. They followed Moses. Now, they didn't know what was going to happen. But there was no turning back. The Egyptian Army was back there! The only way out was to go forward." Stan took a small step forward.

"Okay, watch this now. Moses parted the Red Sea. With his *hand*!" he whispered. "His *hand*!" His outstretched hand hovered over the miracle. We were no longer in the gathering space at First Baptist Church. We were now at the edge of the Red Sea, awestruck, watching the waters divide. Stan stepped back from the edge of the stage, pulling the mic cord up and around him, and stopped near me.

"Okay, look. When I met Dave, I had just done ten years in prison. And I was facing another ten years. I was not where I wanted to be in life. But Dave put a pen in my hand. He told me to write." He gestured toward me, turned to make eye contact, then turned back to face the people. "Dave was my guide. He got me through it. Dave parted the sea of incarceration."

The woman in the front row clutched her heart and closed her eyes in prayer.

"Now, I wasn't seeing a white man doing this. I saw his spirit! God don't look at us the way *we* look at us. He sees our spirit. Right or wrong?"

"Right!" the people told him. Then Stan passed me the mic, winking discreetly as he sat.

I was unsure what to say in my new role as Moses. Then I thought about him writing in prison at my suggestion, and I rose, holding the mic in front of me like a staff. Through writing, you get to create your own world. You make it from yourself and give it to yourself. This is your true dominion.

19
White Guy

Dave

Fall, 2016. "Dave, do you see that guy?" Ronald asked, cupping his hand around my ear. I saw a white guy at two o'clock standing by a red brick building. This could describe just about any student and any building at the University of Richmond.

"That guy?" I gestured.

"Don't point!" Ronald pulled my arm down. I looked at him, then again at the guy.

"Don't stare!" he hissed.

What then? I asked with my eyes.

"He's staring at us," Ronald explained.

There aren't many middle-aged Black men at the University of Richmond who are not in some kind of uniform, working. And so, when Ronald, Terence, Stan, Kelvin, and I walked over the brick pathways and fine-grained lawns with our host, Sylvia, a professor who was leading us to our book event, the guys drew attention in ways that they did not when they came to see me at Virginia Commonwealth University, a more diverse, downtown campus without borders separating it from the rest of the city. Although it is technically in the city, the University of Richmond, is miles away near a country club and the large, stately homes of the West End.

I had not fully registered the difference between the two campuses until Ronald showed me that he was on the outside looking in. How easily I had slipped back into this environment! I grew up in a similar upper-middle-class, white suburb of Connecticut. In Ohio, I attended a similar liberal arts college, also predominantly white and middle-class. Had Ronald and the others strode across my college campus when I was a student, I would have been a little startled, too. In another time and place, I could have been that guy at two o'clock.

But I did not grow up thinking of myself as white. I was raised to think of myself as Italian and Irish. Genealogy, geography, ethnicity, language, culture, food—these were the ways I remember talking about identity—not color. It took some time before I understood what James Baldwin describes as a process of European immigrants becoming Americans. In the old country, he explains, Europeans did not necessarily share the same language, eat the same foods, practice the same religion or politics, and so on. In America, they became what they had never been in Europe. They paid the price of the ticket, as he put it. The price was to become white. "America became white because of the necessity of denying the Black presence, and justifying the Black subjugation."[28] I don't recall paying the price of that ticket. Maybe my parents or grandparents bought it for me? I know that I benefit from being white. In the flux of daily life, though, it is easy to forget the privilege. It isn't something I am conscious of until someone like Ronald makes me see it.

Sylvia led us across campus into one of the older brick buildings where we would be doing our book talk. It was beautiful. An ornate parlor displayed paintings of patriarchs and benefactors of the university. The floor was covered with a large Persian rug. In the corner was a plum-colored Victorian love seat that nobody sat in.

Terence read a piece about growing up in the housing projects with a mother working two or three jobs. Stan read a piece about the prostitute who taught him how to hustle when he was a teen. Ronald, who had returned from Baltimore for this event, read a piece about manipulating a truck driver into sex after selling him crack. And Kelvin read a piece about being in prison at Christmas and hearing his favorite song—"Silent Night" by the Temptations—but refusing to cry. Once a man cries in prison, he explained, he's considered soft.

The stories were raw, relatable, and resonated in each man's unique voice and style of presentation. But in the refined light of the parlor, they seemed untoward. The audience of students and professors mostly looked down or away. Unlike other readings we had given in community centers, bookstores, and churches, where you could feel the emotion of the people listening and see the empathy enlarging their eyes, this group seemed unsure how to feel or how to express what they were feeling. In the Q&A, they cooled the heat of the stories with a spray of ideas: the racist history of public housing, poverty and the catalysts for crime, the agency of sex workers, and the performance of Black masculinity. Good points, all. But they came from the head. It was not clear that they had really heard the guys or felt the stories in their hearts.

After the audience left, Terence, Ronald, and I sat in the plum love seat. Stan and Kelvin stood behind us. Sylvia took our picture. We looked like contestants on a reality TV show.

We made our way to my car. Stan took the passenger seat on the drive home. Kelvin was bent up in the back seat behind me. Terence took the seat behind Stan and began filling the cabin with little quips and jokes. Ronald perched on the hump in the middle and began hand jiving to the music. When he started singing, Kelvin let out a big laugh. We made our way off campus onto Cary Street. Terence leaned out the window and shouted something. And the clown car coasted through the afternoon light back into the inner city.

Stan was the first stop. I parked in the driveway of his sister's house, where he was staying. He got out, then turned back to face the three guys in the back seat. "All right, one of you has to come up here and sit with Dave." From the rearview mirror, I saw heads turning and eyes inquiring—which one?

"Yeah, don't make it look like I'm the chauffeur," I said, taking my place in whatever joke might be forming.

"No, Dave. That's not it. Not at all," Stan said. "If you drive this car down Cary into the Fan by VCU, with these three in the back, someone's gonna think this is a robbery and one of them got a gun." Oh, how they laughed! Oh, how it hurt. I had forgotten again.

20

Soil Sample

Stan

Upon my release in October of 2015, I went searching for the perfect environment in which to grow. Like a beautiful African violet, I would need the right amount of sun and shade to become bountiful and strong. My release from prison became my season to transplant my life from a small, shallow pot of confinement to the vast wilderness of society. Release took years to crystallize. It was and continues to be a slow process. Seconds turn into minutes. Minutes into hours. Hours into days. Days into months. Months into years. I spent ten years in prison. But when I got out, I was not really free.

When I was a young man, I used to work for Lawn Doctor. Do you remember their trucks? They have the man with the green thumb on his hat. That was me. I have my pesticide, herbicide, and fungicide licenses. I'm a bona fide and certified master gardener, registered at Southern States Corporation. I have spent many years in and out of the Virginia Department of Corrections applying my knowledge about landscaping, plants, and shrub material. Before planting anything, I would start by testing the pH level of the soil. Plants and people have a lot in common. We both need a healthy environment to support our collective and individual growth.

Here is my enigma: What I knew, I did not apply to my own life. I did not think to test the soil into which I transplanted myself. The main nutrient that I needed to grow was love. Honestly, I did more dying than living in this new environment called free society.

When I got out, *Writing Our Way Out* had just been released and was gaining traction in terms of book readings and speaking events around

Richmond. The Black Iris Gallery, First Baptist Church, University of Richmond, VCU, Georgetown University in DC. The list goes on and on. The book gave all of us something to gloat about. I found myself addressing and sharing before waves of interesting people. Outwardly, I had it going on, driving around in my Infiniti G35, wearing dishwasher clothes by day and designer suits in the moonlight. I was giving talks as a published author. It was reentry on a positive note.

But with all the smiles and eyes on me, I still found myself lonely for a woman. A stunning, vibrant woman who would consume my mind, body, and soul. A woman I would be smitten with. Yet most of the females I was meeting didn't seem to understand how to be a partner. After a mere introduction, I would be given a set of rules to comply with, no exceptions. I got burnt out trying to fulfill other people's objectives.

Women were designed to be in a relationship. Society, on the other hand, has abated Black family relationships in exchange for prizing singleness, educational status, and earnings. Men are supposed to help their so-called partner live above their financial means. Nails must be done weekly. Hairdos weekly. Designer bags. Designer clothes. There are no plans for a future together.

The women I met when I got out were just as convoluted as I was, just as guarded. You want me to be genuine? You want me to be kind? You want me to be straightforward, strong, vulnerable? How? I'm looking at this helmet on your head—a weave or a wig, whatever you want to call it. You won't be authentic. You have all these criteria that I have to live by, but I don't even know what you look like without that helmet on your head. How can I take you seriously?

After a lot of dice rolls, I recoiled away from the idea of a partner. Instead, I took up residency in the familiar old prison of the past, that one-bedroom apartment where my father abandoned me as a child in total isolation, where no person can enter but at the cost of not being able to leave.

21
My First Love

Naji

In 2009, Cassandra, my first love, was the only source of light in the hell that had become my life. I had lost her for about twenty years when my addiction got the better of me and got me locked up over and over again. The sense of loss I felt when we parted was indescribable. Searching for her and wondering about her life became almost a daily ritual for me. Through social media, I discovered she was now living in California, and we quickly rekindled online what we once shared in person.

I shared with Cassandra that I was depressed about losing my grandmother and not getting the closure I so desperately needed, dropping out of school, and just being isolated with no prospects in Arizona. However, selfishness, shame, and embarrassment kept me from informing her that I was actively using cocaine. I regret that decision to this day. My silence about my issues deprived her of the right to make an informed decision about entering into a serious relationship with me. I took that from her, and I justified it by convincing myself that she was the answer. She would fill this empty crater in my soul. I felt that with her back in my life, I would definitely get myself together. The repercussions for her if I failed never crossed my mind.

Seeing my pain, this beautiful woman decided to uproot herself and her kids from their lives to rescue me from the chaos of my own. She left California and met up with me in Arizona. Quickly, the stress of being the head of a ready-made family, along with the mountain of other problems I was dealing with, began to eat away at my resolve. I became unmotivated to find employment or pursue any goals. I retreated into myself and my addiction. Doing my best to conceal it, my behavior became strange and erratic. It was obvious to Cassandra that something was wrong, but I ignored the telltale signs that I was slipping further away from the relationship I had been silently praying for, for years. Eventually, I gave dirty urine to my probation officer. In my insanity, I did this twice more in less than six months. My PO had no choice but to violate me.

I was extradited back to Virginia to answer for my actions. I had no choice but to leave Cassandra and the kids. I felt like a complete piece of shit! On the plane ride back to Virginia, I made a solid promise to myself that I was not going to fail Cassandra; that I was going to utilize my time in jail wisely; and that I was going to figure out a way to not be the same person I was when I came in. I didn't know exactly how I was going to accomplish this, but I knew I needed to do something.

I was disgusted with myself for how I'd treated her and the kids and for where my life was at that point in time overall. I was sick to death of the drug-criminal lifestyle and what it had reduced me to. My primary concern was how I was going to rectify the pain I had caused my family. How was I going to rebuild the trust I'd completely destroyed? Trust that was so unselfishly given. Trust that I had selfishly squandered in a pitiful drug-induced haze.

For the first time, I realized that changing people, places, and things wasn't enough to change the thoughts and behaviors that guided my actions. I needed to change my concept of myself and take action to better our lives. Being a man to me at that point in my life meant more than anything, being a provider—something I'd failed at miserably. I believed I could redeem myself by becoming a successful entrepreneur. I would be able to make Cassandra happy by putting us in a position to be financially independent. My ultimate plan was to lead my family out of poverty and into the life we both dreamed of. With everything in my soul, I wanted to give Cassandra the life she deserved. I needed her to look at me again with adoration in her eyes, marveling at the strength, sacrifice, and dedication I had to overcome my challenges to make our lives better.

I ended up at St. Brides Correctional Center for approximately eighteen months. I got straight to work. I went to the library to see what resources were available. I wanted to know how to start a business. I found a book on business structure for dummies, and I spent every waking moment reading it and taking notes. I taught myself about corporations and their different structures. LLCs, sole-proprietorships, S corps, for-profit, and nonprofit organizations. I consumed anything I could get my hands on that talked about business. As I studied, so many different ideas popped into my head about what I could actually start.

I assessed my talents and came up with even more ideas. The more I learned, the more determined I became. I knew that I was going to make something of myself. I could see the future ahead of me clearly. I would get on the phone with Cassandra, so excited to share with her what I was learning. I wanted desperately for her to jump on board with me. I felt this door opening, and I knew if I could paint the picture for her and get her to see it as I did, we would be well on our way!

Being incarcerated and having a loved one on the outside is a very difficult thing for both people. Cassandra had bills to pay. She had the kids to take care of. She had work and the responsibilities that came along with that. And she was doing this by herself, not to mention the fact that she was lonely and didn't have me there when she needed help with all the things that caused her stress. I was wondering why,vwhen I got on the phone with her and would tell her how motivated I was and how I needed her to get on board with me, she didn't seem to share my enthusiasm. To me, it felt as though she just wanted to stay in the poverty trap she was in.

I remember asking her on numerous occasions to pull up information for me on her computer, info that I couldn't get from the library at the penitentiary, and send it to me so that I could further my education. She would always respond that she would do it, but I never received anything from her. I would question her about it, and I would always get the same answer. She didn't have enough time, or she was tired, or she couldn't find the information I was looking for. This frustrated me to no end. Here I was trying to make something of myself and to raise my family out of poverty, and my partner wasn't in the game.

I remember telling her that I didn't want to come out the same individual I was when I went in. I explained that I was spending every waking moment educating myself so that when I hit the ground, I wouldn't have to get a low-end, dead-end job working for somebody else when I could be working for myself and for us. It's one of the key points that I tried to get her to understand: that she didn't have to work for anybody else, something she really hated doing. That I would do everything in my power to free her from a nine-to-five job. But she just didn't get it.

I would later come to understand she was concerned about my ability to do any of this. Her confidence in me was damaged due to my lack of consistency. She had not seen this type of drive from me at any other point in our relationship and wasn't willing to go out on a limb and take the chance that I was asking her to take. Talk is cheap, and I believe she wanted to see me start things on my own, to lead so she could follow, which was understandable, considering, but I still needed her full support. We were at odds on this issue, and together we got nothing accomplished.

At the end of my time, I was released and moved in with Cassandra, who had gotten a place in Hampton, Virginia. As you might imagine, I tried to maintain the enthusiasm that I had while in the system, but I quickly shorted myself out. I got a dead-end job at a restaurant. Then I got another. I hated life. Nothing that I wanted to achieve, nothing that I had dreamed about, was coming to pass. In fact, things were going quickly in the opposite direction.

Depression set in. I returned to active use. I secretly blamed Cassandra for what I was going through. I thought if she had just provided me with the information that I needed, I could have educated myself and found out about loans and how to achieve funding for these businesses that I wanted to start, and we would have been on our way. I was delusional. The problem was always my inability to accept life on life's terms, along with my complete lack of understanding of my past trauma, how I was affected by it, and what I needed to do to overcome it.

I loved Cassandra dearly, but I felt like a complete failure in her eyes, so I began to hang out in the streets again. We would frequently get into arguments about my absence from home. I would stay out in the streets sometimes for days before coming home with a lie and an excuse. I had completely removed myself, physically and emotionally, from our relationship. At one point, I snuck out of the house and stole her car so that I could make a drug run, and the car was stolen by a fellow addict. The car was recovered, but my relationship had fallen apart completely, and I was the one to blame.

Greater lapses in judgment followed. Alcohol destroyed my natural ability to correct myself. I became someone I didn't recognize. After a major blowout, Cassandra had had enough and ended our relationship. I was crushed, but I couldn't blame her. I couldn't explain myself, and she didn't want to hear it anymore. I was disgusted with how I had handled things and, in shame, I left.

22
Grit

Dave

Spring, 2017. It was dark in The Local. A little dank. Stan sat at a little table in the back with a cup of coffee on a saucer. With his shirt unbuttoned into a small V and a gold chain resting on his chest, he looked less like the dishwasher at an Irish bar than someone biding his time before the real business began.

"What's happening, Dave?" he called out over a thumping beat better suited for late night than the dead of the afternoon. He caught the attention of the bartender and made a little twisting motion with his fingers. She lowered the music.

"Just thought I'd stop in to see how my coauthors are getting along as coworkers."

"Yeah, no doubt."

I nodded toward the kitchen. "Is he back there?"

Stan got up and pushed through the saloon doors. A moment later, Naji appeared in a long white apron with a tiny spiral notebook.

"How's that roasted red pepper soup coming?" Stan asked.

"It's coming." Naji looked at the notebook, up at the ceiling, then back at the notebook and cursed.

"Boss is making him memorize the menu," Stan explained.

"The cooking is easy. It's the memorizing!" Naji seemed torn between the frustration of memorizing and the annoyance of having a boss who was making him memorize.

He had not moved to Richmond from Hampton to make soup. He wanted to do more book events, especially the paid events. At first, there was no money in these events because I had not thought to ask for it. For me, the purpose of the events was to keep the collective together, spread our message, and sell more books. But after seeing how little money we made from book royalties and seeing my coauthors forever struggling to make enough money to live, I began asking our hosts for honoraria.

"So, Dave—when's the next event?" Naji asked.

"Not sure yet. I've got some calls and emails out. Waiting to hear back."

He sighed, then asked if I could give him a ride. He had an application to turn in for a kitchen position at Waffle House. He needed a second job. He needed more money. He only had enough in his pocket for a week at the motel.

The sky darkened as we drove west down Broad Street. I opened the windows. A breeze passed between us. Naji tapped a pack of Newports against his palm in a steady beat. Then he broke the silence.

"What kind of jobs could I get writing?"

Great question. He was a natural. From the thick descriptions to the intense reflections, he had a way of immersing the reader in his world. I noticed it from the very beginning, when I met him in jail. But this was also a hard question. Students asked it, too. The problem was that I did not know many people who were paid to write. Most of the writers I knew were professors. Their money came from teaching.

"Have you considered journalism?"

"Dave, I'm considering whatever puts bread on the table, you know what I'm saying?" It began to rain. We rolled up the windows. I parked in front of the Waffle House and watched him sprint in with the application rolled into a tight cylinder. When he got back, his shirt was blotched with water.

"Where to?"

"Back to The Local."

"You're not staying at the motel?"

"Nah, Dave. I need that money. There's an apartment above the bar. The guys living there said I could crash on the couch."

We drove in silence. Just the beat of the wipers. A few minutes later, we parked by the neon green, four-leaf clover light of The Local and waited for a lull in the storm. A woman smoked under the awning. Two couples came out of the door, cursed the rain, then gave in to the hilarity of getting soaked. Three guys lunged across the street, dodging cars, laughing and shouting to each other as they went. An old man in frayed khakis sipped a forty under the roof of the 7-Eleven. His face was weathered and creased like a cowboy's.

"I love this," Naji said from a reverie. I wrinkled my face. What did he love? He gestured to the people out there beyond the windshield.

"This scene. These people, doing who knows what, going who knows where. All these stories starting in the middle. And no one knows I've just joined." He unbuckled his seat belt and turned to face me.

"I know you've done a lot for me today, Dave, and I want to thank you. But do you think you can do one more thing for me?" His face was slender and precise, his eyes steady on mine.

"Can you lend me ten dollars so I can go into that 7-Eleven and get me something to eat?" Headlights from the passing cars illuminated his eyes, then disappeared, leaving us in the shadows. I tried to see what I might be missing.

"I only get to eat when I'm on shift." He jabbed his thumb toward The Local. "I'm off now." I gave him ten dollars.

Later that week, I called him on my walk through the park by my house. I had good news. We were a finalist at two big universities for their common book programs. Getting a book adopted by one of these programs would mean selling thousands of books at once. This, in turn, would mean a substantial royalty check. It would also mean bigger speaking fees.

As I shared the news, Naji became intensely alert, asking follow-up questions about what kind of money we were talking about and the timetable for a payout. He was like a prospector watching me swing a pickaxe. I was still swinging, but he was already seeing flecks of gold flittering in the air. Most of our competitors were authors with books from big New York presses. People with name recognition. I was more impressed that we had managed to become finalists without an agent or publicist and with a book from a small, local press. Months later, I would have to tell him and the others that our book had not been selected.

***

Stan was at his usual table, scribbling on scratch paper with a stubby pencil, his reading glasses halfway down his nose. He looked like a bookie getting ready to make a tough call. The bartender was laughing in a voice loud enough to cut over the power chords of the metal she was playing. Stan called her name, pinched his fingers and twisted, and the wall of sound came down.

"What's happening, Dave?"

"I got us an event. A keynote at the READ Center."

"Okay, cool." He looked up and waited for me to explain.

"Local organization. They teach people how to read. Turns out some of the teachers have been using *Writing Our Way Out*."

"Go on now!"

"They felt they could get their students reading if they gave them stories that they could relate to. It could be that your story is the first story some of these folks have ever read."

"Damn!" He pounded the table and pushed away the pencil and paper. "That's humbling, Dave, for real. I never thought something I wrote could help someone like that." I hadn't either.

"Hey, where's Naji? I want to tell him, too."

"Okay, look." He straightened up. "About that. Did he tell you about crashing on that couch upstairs?" I braced myself.

"Well, it turns out that couch belongs to two young cats, VCU students, I think. And they're into cocaine. And he's coming in late, like let me have some." My heart skipped ahead of the conversation. Immediately, I thought about the ten dollars I had given Naji the other day.

"Anyway, like I told him, right? They're not your friends. They're not thinking of you! You're just crashing there."

"So, what happened?"

"He split."

"Back to the motel?"

"Nah. Left Richmond. Nothing keeping him here."

"He had this job!"

"Couldn't memorize the menu. The boss let him go."

"What about the Waffle House?"

"He took the bus back to Hampton last night." I imagined him on a bus, looking out into the void from a window seat, his dreams of making it as a writer receding into the evening.

"So, look—about this literacy center. Are they taking new people?"

"Probably, yeah. Why?"

"What are you doing Saturday?"

I picked up Stan on Saturday. He wanted to introduce me to his niece in elementary school, who was having trouble reading. He conceded that he did not know her well; he was just starting to get to know her family. Until he got out of prison, he had not even met them. Stan was adopted. The

Craddocks were the only family he knew. But while writing his memoir, he began wondering about his birth family. A friend did the research for him and relayed the information in a letter. In prison, he learned that his birth mother was dead. There was no record of his father. But from these clues, he learned his birth identity. His last name was Jackson. His first name was Maurice. He had a brother, Michael, a sister, Sharmane, and this niece, a little girl in fifth grade.

We parked and began to stroll toward the apartment. "So, I told Sharmane, right? Dave's got a PhD in English! *A PhD!* He'll know what to do." I did not know how to explain that a PhD in English did not prepare a person to teach reading to children. But when I imagined it from his point of view, it did seem logical. Wasn't the PhD the highest degree you could get? Weren't little kids reading at a lower level than college students?

He knocked on the door. A woman's voice shouted to come in, where we found Sharmane filling a large part of the sectional. A TV was turned up loud, playing *The Price Is Right*. She smiled when she saw Stan, but struggled to get up. He moved close to her, bent his knees, and offered his hand.

"C'mon, mama," he commanded. She grabbed his hand. Slowly, he shifted his weight from right to left. After several long seconds, she rose and stood on her own, embraced Stan, greeted me, then began to tell me about Shanice.

"She has a developmental delay," she explained. "She's in fifth grade. But she reads at a first-grade level."

"Does she have an Individual Education Plan?"

"Yes, but they don't follow it! I'm so scared, Dr. Coogan! She graduates from elementary school next year, and these teachers keep promoting her to the next grade. I don't know what else to do."

"How did she get the developmental delay?" I asked. Sharmane looked at me, then at Stan, turned away, embarrassed, and hid her face in her hands.

"I'm sorry. It's none of my business."

"It's okay, Dr. Coogan. I don't mind telling you. It's just hard." She took a big sniff, found a tissue, and wiped her eyes. "Her mother used to blow her marijuana smoke into the baby's face. When I found out, I took custody." Stan let out an expressive grunt that somehow managed to condemn the mother while praising his sister.

"Is she here?"

Sharmane took a step around me to shout down the hallway.

"Shanice! Come here, baby. Your uncle Stan's here." Shanice came running into the room and into Stan, who was crouched down now, arms open to receive her. Sharmane introduced me as Dr. Coogan, a VCU professor here to help her with her reading. Then all three of them were looking at me as if a real family doctor had come to make a house call.

I told Shanice to bring me all of her books. I asked Sharmane to get me some paper and a pencil, but she was already sitting again, watching the game show, so she told Stan where to find them in the kitchen. He came back with her recipe book and a pen. Shanice returned with Dr. Seuss's *Green Eggs and Ham,* then threw herself in front of the TV. I asked Sharmane to mute the show.

"Is this the only book you have?" I was hoping to see the books she was struggling to read, something from school.

"The others are at her father's house," Sharmane explained.

"Oh, okay," I asked Shanice to read me *Green Eggs and Ham*. She smiled that little kid smile that says I am about to show off something I know how to do. She knew the story well. A little too well. She was turning the pages before she had finished reading what was on them. At one point, she was not looking at the page while telling me the story, but at the TV. I asked Sharmane to turn off the show. Then I asked Shanice to start again. With nothing else to distract them, Sharmane and Stan were forced to listen to Shanice and me.

"Okay, let's play a game," I suggested, raising my eyebrows. "I'm going to take away some of the words with my thumb, and you have to read the story by just saying the words you can see. It will be silly." She agreed. Her ponytail was tightly drawn and tied with a red jewel. She reached up to adjust it, then looked up at me. Ready. She read the story the way it was written, including all of the random words I had covered up. When I pointed out that she had not read the story the new way, she started to panic. She did not want to disappoint me. I didn't want her to cry. But by now, I wasn't sure which words she could identify. She must have memorized the book. As I scrambled to figure out the next step, the door creaked.

"Oh, that's her father come to get her," Sharmane said. He walked into the room without greeting anyone or asking who the white guy was sitting right next to his daughter. He kept his sunglasses on, grabbed the remote, turned the game show on, and sat down next to Stan. When he set down the remote, Stan picked it up, turned off the TV, told him who I was, and what we were doing to help Shanice. He shrugged and took out his phone.

"Hey, man, you got books for your daughter up in the house?" Stan asked.

"Yeah."

"Where they at?"

"In the closet." Stan looked down at Shanice.

"Do you have your books in your closet?"

"I got 'em in mines," the father said.

"Okay, look!" Stan said, leaning forward, elbows on his knees. "I know you're *busy*, and all that, but your girl needs her books in her room. Can you get that done today?"

The man looked up from his phone, mumbled something reassuring enough to get the tough guy out of his face, but cool enough to show he wasn't taking orders. Then his phone rang. He took the call out on the front porch.

"He can't read," Sharmane whispered to me once he was outside. "He's ashamed to admit it." She paused again to collect her feelings. "I know my baby wants to do better in school, but I think she feels like if she does, she's going to lose him. At least, that's how I see it." Stan gave another one of those expressive grunts that encapsulated the dilemma.

"You know, Stan and I are going to be doing an event at the READ Center next month. They teach adults how to read. They could help him, if he's willing," I said, gesturing to the front porch. Her eyes grew wide and hopeful.

"If he can get into reading, they could make that a part of their relationship. I'll get some info to Stan to bring to you. Okay?" Sharmane nodded quickly, thanking me over and over. The father finished his call and returned to the living room to sink into the couch. Stan and I turned to leave. I tried to say goodbye to Shanice, but she was already leaning deep into her father's arms. He was reaching for the remote.

It took a few weeks before I could get Naji on the phone. I did not ask him about the couch or the cocaine, or the ten dollars. I asked him if he still wanted to be a writer. He did. I suggested there might be a way to do it from Hampton. He could pitch to the Marshall Project, a national organization reporting on the criminal justice system. They paid for submissions, and they wanted formerly incarcerated people to write for them. I had met one of the editors.

"Okay, set it up," he said. Annoyance crept in. Couldn't he just contact the editor himself? Why did he need me to set it up? Then I thought about it: Had I not already set myself up as his agent for speaking events? Did I not have the time to write an email? Of course I did. A few rounds of emails later, the editor commissioned Naji to write a piece on the automatic restoration of voting rights for felons in Virginia. At this point, I excused myself from the email thread and patted myself on the back. If he could start writing for a good list of publications along these lines, maybe he could build a resume and look for a full-time job as a reporter.

I called Naji a few weeks later to see if the piece had been published. He did not know. He had lost his phone and didn't have reliable access to a computer. He had a new phone now, the one he was using to talk to me, and he had found a library with computers. But he was busy looking for another restaurant job. He still wanted to be a writer. But the vision seemed less like a beacon guiding him than an escape hatch he could not pry open.

Naji had talent. But Angela Duckworth has argued that the main driver of achievement is not talent, but grit. In order to achieve, a person's talent needs to be honed into a skill. The person also needs a growth mindset and a long-term vision of success.[30] Duckworth is a psychologist who developed her theory by analyzing the way high-achieving people handle themselves in spelling bees, military training, and elite consulting firms.

In his critique of Duckworth's book, David Denby notes that most of these case studies, where people exhibit grit, are removed from life the way most people live it. Few tasks in life are as narrowly proscribed as a spelling bee. Life is filled with overlapping tasks that are diverse and demanding socially, intellectually, and technically. Navigating them requires improvisation skills, along with confidence, a sense of self-worth, and a support structure[31]—none of which come easy when a person is suffering psychologically from multiple layers of trauma, as Naji was.

Duckworth acknowledges this larger cultural framing of grit in a footnote in her book. She writes, "Trauma is not the royal road to grit. On the contrary, it's well documented that poverty, discrimination, and uncertainty can have a crushing effect on physical health, psychological well-being, and character development."[32] But the popularity of her work, particularly as it has been applied to struggling, under-resourced communities, begs the question: Do traumatized people need to develop more grit to change their lives, or does society need to change so that traumatized people have a better chance at developing grit?

When the READ Center event came up, I called Naji to invite him to participate. He told me that Cassandra could drive him, but she needed gas money. She didn't get paid until the week after the event. He didn't have any money, so he asked if I could send him the honorarium ahead of time. I sent him the fifty dollars. He never showed up. I called the next day. He told me that he had gotten the money from Western Union, but when he walked out of the place, he got robbed.

"What?"

"It's fine. I'm fine now. I've been through worse, believe me."

Later, I texted Cassandra to ask how he was doing—how they were both doing—after the robbery. That text string lasted for several days. Twenty dollars had gone missing from her purse. The old printer she had not used in a while was also missing. Then there was the time she heard the door opening in the middle of the night. It woke her up. At first, she thought it was a robbery. It was just him coming home late again and collapsing on the couch.

She did not believe he had been robbed the other night. She thought he had used that money to get high, just like he had sold her things to get high. She was tired of asking him if he had gone out looking for a job. Whenever she left for work, he was there on the couch, half-awake, reaching for the remote. When she came back, he was gone.

23
To Tell the Story

Dave

Fall, 2017. "I think we passed it, Dave." I pulled over to look at the address on the piece of paper I'd given Stan. "I think it's back there in that little plaza," he said. I looked out the back window. I could see a dentist's office, a bistro, and a gas station. I didn't see any address numbers or the name of the place we're looking for.

"All right, I'm confused," I said, turning the car around. "I'm going to go into that plaza and talk to the people in the gas station." We parked and walked into the shop connected to the garage. At the counter, I asked the girl by the register if she knew anything about the Village Exxon Book Club. She looked up from her magazine and pointed to a greasy wooden door. I looked at Stan. His face was blank. I looked back at the girl again to confirm. She just stared at me like, What?

I opened the door and walked through. Natural light flooded the bay. The underside of a car was exposed on a lift. Heavy tools hung on the wall behind it. A woman with a cherubic face greeted us and led us to a table arrayed with crackers and fruit. Nearby, the book club members were taking their places in folding chairs arranged in a circle near the car. I nibbled some melon. Stan poured a lemonade. The air smelled densely metallic. When the woman turned away to greet someone, Stan gave me an amused smile. Since the book was published, we had been to fine churches and elite universities. We had spoken at schools, bookstores, nonprofits, art galleries, and professional societies. We had never done an event in a garage.

We took our seats. The woman who greeted us at the door welcomed us officially to the Village Exxon Book Club. The people of the club smiled sweetly and clapped. When I was called on to speak, I explained why I started the writing class at the jail where I met Stan. Then Stan read the story of his father abandoning him as a teenager to live in a one-bedroom apartment on Grace Street. A prostitute befriends him. She does not just give him sex, he explained, but the intimacy of her thoughts. She teaches him how to hustle and steal. She tells him to use people before they use you. He is grateful. He is lonely. He misses his mother's cooking. He misses the family photos on the wall. He wonders what he could have done that was so bad his father left him to fend for himself.

Stan read and read until the underside of his life was exposed up there on the lift of our imagination. Then he closed the book. Specks of dust descended into the shared space of the circle. The man next to me let out a raspy sigh. The woman with blonde-grey hair sitting across from me opened her mouth to speak, but appeared stuck, cathecting. The people of the club seemed to be hunting for the right tool to probe the parts of his life, to diagnose the problem, and work toward a solution. But no one made a move.

"What did it feel like?" the woman with the blonde-grey hair finally asked. "What did it feel like to write about that time of your life?" Stan looked down, gathering his thoughts, then lifted his head to meet her gaze.

"You know that feeling you get when you know you're going to be sick?" Her hand found her face, covering her mouth. "It was like that. Regurgitation. I had to get rid of all that bile inside."

It is one thing to write through those memories alone, to stick your fingers down your throat until the story comes up. It's another thing to publish it, and still another to read it aloud to strangers. There is a doubling. You are no longer the story that you wrote. You are no longer straining over the toilet for the first time. But then you open the book. You begin convulsing in a ritual heave until the memories spill all over the smooth concrete of some mechanic's garage.

Roger Luckhurst describes the experience of reliving trauma as a circling "around a shattering event, from which self-knowledge arrives late, if at all, and with an uncomfortable awareness of the frangibility of the self."[33] Each time you orbit yourself, you realize how fragile that self once was and maybe still is. If you could only stop circling around it, stop talking about it, maybe the pain would go away?

* * *

I met Ronald outside the hotel. He was smoking nervously, his arm dropping and rising like a puppet. The hotel meeting room where he was going to speak was overlit and crowded. Straight-back chairs had been pressed together, forming something like a bench with backs. The benches were filled with women from the Virginia Sexual & Domestic Violence Action Alliance—women who, if they had not experienced sexual violence, were allies of those who had: therapists, researchers, policy makers, and advocates.

"Good evening, everybody," Ronald said with a smile. The women returned his warm greeting. But when he began reading his story, the air clogged with concern.

He was in elementary school when older girls in the neighborhood forced him and another boy into an alley and commanded them to fellate each other. He told no one. Yet somehow, he felt people knew. The next week, while playing hide-and-seek with another boy, the boy took out his penis and told Ronald to put it in his mouth. When he did, the boy tried to piss in it. Ronald stayed indoors for a week. When he could not stand the isolation any longer, he went out looking for the one he played hide and seek with, but found his older brother at home instead. He told the brother he wanted to feel it inside him, thinking in his mouth, but the brother began to rape him anally.

As he read, the women watched him fiercely, telegraphing messages. Thoughts were flowing unhindered from their foreheads. They were sorry. They were angry. They were worried that he was still suffering. They were crying. They were analyzing. They were resolved to find new ways of advocating for people like him. He heard the chorus of emotion. It was too much. He broke down.

"I'm sorry," he said as he turned the book over and turned away from the podium to cry. He took a deep breath, covering his face with one hand.

"Take your time," a woman in the front row suggested. Someone handed him a tissue. The seconds swelled into a fat minute. He turned to face the microphone again. I caught a shiver of guilt for arranging this event.

"This is harder than I thought," Ronald told them. He wiped a tear. I offered to read for him. He smiled and told me, No, it's okay. He could do it. He wanted to do it.

Soon, he was out of his early childhood experiences and into his adolescent angst. He came out. He declared his school days over and began an extended rebellion that led him to ever more risky situations involving sex, drugs, stolen cars, jail cells, suicide attempts, and the deliverance of prayer. When he finished the story, he assured the women that today he is okay. Today, he no longer hides in silence.

"I am a survivor of sexual assault, but also a survivor of the criminal justice system. I am no longer ashamed to tell my story."

The applause was overwhelming. I was awestruck, both by his courage and this reception. A cluster of women approached Ronald by the podium when the event ended. They hugged him and confided in him. Though I could not hear it all, I could see from their faces and hear from their tones that they were assuring him they knew the pain of the memory and the pain of reliving it, but also the relief of having released it. It was a vexing kind of freedom. To be free of the story, you have to tell the story.

24

Lower Vibration, Higher Vibration

Stan

It is said that one hit is too many and a thousand cannot quench the addiction. But it goes deeper than that. With each hit of crack, I fall deeper and deeper into its arms. We spend hours together. Addiction becomes my soulmate, my purpose for living as well as dying, it seems.

Keys and tools are needed to unlock the cell doors of one's demonic spirit. I am stepping into the lower realm of myself now. My lower vibration. This is where the demonic spirit dwells in me. Stem char and lighter supplement this demonic brew. Now the main ingredient can be added. I put crack cocaine into the char-packed stem, taking a few test runs of flicking my lighter to ensure it works correctly.

Next, my shutdown list can be activated. All doors that could lead to help must be boarded up. Total isolation must be achieved as I ignite this fuse to my demise. The flame of my Bic lighter subdues my eyes. It dances to my delight while engaging with the crack stuffed in the stem. I inhale, filling my lungs and what seems like every cell in my body. A hissing sound can be heard as the flame melts the crack. I find myself pausing for a moment before I exhale to feel the full effect before it is released, this demonic spirit that dwells in me.

I stand up and look at myself in the mirror. Truly, Stan's reflection has disappeared. I see the demon dance as it tortures my soul without remorse. Yet again and again, Bic lighter in hand, stem filled with crack, I inhale with pleasure. I am dying. I am surrendering without a fight. Addiction confines, binds, and helps me bleed out to the point of flatline.

Now think about it. If you get sick enough or hurt enough, where do they take you? The hospital. What do they do? Put drugs in you to manage the pain. But what about the low-income person who doesn't have insurance? How do they manage the pain? They manage their pain with fentanyl. They manage their pain with heroin. They manage their pain with coke. They manage their pain with alcohol. They manage their pain with marijuana. They manage their pain with abuse.

In my neighborhood, that's how they do it. That's how they try to fix their broken parts. And that's really all you see. The broken parts. Distress, anguish, hopelessness. You walk out the front door, and all you see are body parts, character parts, lying all around you.

In our book events, I had an opportunity to step outside my addiction and my problems to seek my higher vibration. I enjoy interacting. I got high on the reality that people do care. Not all of them. But some of the people in those rooms were really concerned or curious about our frame of mind. Not just mine, but the collective group: Writing Our Way Out. The energy was good.

I remember one guy in the front row asking, When did you start trusting Coogan? I told him, yeah, I knew exactly when. It was when he brought that banana bread into the jail. That was when we became blood brothers. He showed me that, even though the jail rules said no outside food, he knew that the rule of humanity was greater than any law. How could you not identify? He came over to the criminal side, right where I was.

One of the best events we did was when we went to Deep Meadow Correctional Center. Even though I had never met any of those guys, I knew my audience. I knew I could communicate with them. All I had to do was get out of my head and go to my heart. That's fulfilling. I had the opportunity to spill some stuff, to regurgitate some stuff. And I knew that everything I was saying was felt. It's the same damn story in every prison. It's my story. We all succumb to our lower vibrations at times. But we all have a higher vibration we can tune into if we listen closely enough.

25

Cognitive Dissonance

Dave

Winter, 2017. Headphones coiled around Dean's neck. A microphone jutted up to his lip. The lighting was sparse. The walls were muffled. The producer in the sound booth wore a red bandana. Brown-grey hair fell to his shoulders. Somehow, this made it feel like a real studio—like we were rock stars, making an audiobook of *Writing Our Way Out*.

Kelvin arrived in a grey tracksuit just as Dean was getting ready to record. The producer tapped the glass. Kelvin and I joined him in the booth. Dean read a story about the time he got shot. It's his last scene in the book: He struggles to breathe as he bleeds in the street. He thinks about revenge. In his younger days, he would have had it! Then he thinks about his daughter and the baby on the way. He has to hold on. He has to believe. But it's hard to breathe!

Through the glass, I saw not one but several Deans. It was like looking through a prism. There was the Dean who wrote that scene at the jail in 2006. Then there was the Dean, who had been arrested and incarcerated in 2013 for selling drugs again, the one I had visited in jail. And there was the Dean right here, reading about his original resolve to quit the streets after getting shot.

When Dean was incarcerated again for selling marijuana in 2013, I was pushed off balance. How could he go back into the narrative that he had disavowed in the book? Was I wrong to have believed him the first time that he wanted to steer clear of the streets so that he could be a better father?

Cognitive dissonance—the presence of two contradictory thoughts at one time—irritates belief. Scratching just makes it worse. The new thought cannot be explained with reference to the old thought. Only one can be true. In order to reduce the discomfort of contradiction, you can rationalize away the new thought, minimize it, subordinate it to some other thought, or rename it in such a way that changes its meaning. A new cognitive element must be added or taken away. Something has to give.[34]

In 2013, two US states made the recreational use of marijuana legal. Virginia was not one of them. In 2016, nine states had legalized.[35] Virginia was still not one of them. The problem was not with Dean, I reasoned, but with this patchwork of state laws that enabled some Americans to use marijuana and profit from it, while others were imprisoned for it. Most of the ones who were profiting were white. They had access to capital. Most of those getting imprisoned were Black and poor.[36] This was no boon for my sense of justice. But it was a balm for my cognitive dissonance.

Dean was still reading when my phone buzzed. I stepped out of the booth and began walking down a long hall to carry my voice away from the session. It was Stan.

"I'm not going to make it, Dave." This was strange. Stan was punctual for all of our events. Most times, he was early. I began steeling myself for the story.

"I was at a bar last night," he began. "A dude came in. We got to talking. And you know, his job situation is no different from mine. Then he tells me, right? I know a place on Monument Avenue with a big flat screen TV. 'I know where it's at,' he kept saying. 'The people aren't home. All we have to do is pull it off the wall. Split out the back. Simple.'"

It was simple . . . for the police. They got his fingerprints off the wall of the apartment. There was a warrant out for his arrest. I felt my neck swelling. Adrenaline was coursing through my veins and up my spine into my head.

"Who was this dude?"

"Just a dude."

"Describe him."

"I don't look too closely at dudes, Dave."

"What was his name?"

"Didn't give one."

"Were you high?"

"I was under the influence."

Okay, but which substance? Stan was not much more than a social drinker. Weed was a possibility, but weed didn't make him steal. Weed gave him what he called Picasso thoughts. Weed opened his portals of consciousness. There was only one other option. If cocaine was not in his body at the bar, it was in his scheming to fence a TV to get cocaine into his body.

"What are you going to do?"

"Lay low."

"For how long, though?"

He paused as he selected the image to explain this.

"You ever watch the ocean from shore? That'll be me. I'm just going to recede like the tide. Little by little until I'm gone."

It sounded like he was saying goodbye—to me, to *Writing Our Way Out*, to Richmond, his brothers in the book, everything. Then he grew defiant. "And if any police try to pull me out of that tide? Man, I'll pull them in with me!"

"What?"

"I'm not going back to prison, Dave. I'm just not." Prison was a possibility. Stealing to get money to buy cocaine had led him to prison before. When I met Stan in 2006, he had just finished serving ten years for charges related to his addiction. He'd been free for just under a year before he got arrested for a string of larcenies, which led to another ten years. It was now 2016. Once again, he had been out for just under a year. He was right on time for another prison term.

"I'll call tomorrow," Stan said. "Might be a few days, actually. I need to get a new phone."

I went back to the sound booth. Dean was finished reading. Kelvin had joined him by the little table and was trying on the headphones. They were looking through the book to find Kelvin's pieces. When I entered the room, I released a stream of confusion, worry, embarrassment, and anger. Kelvin grew concerned, as much for me as for Stan. Dean seemed more circumspect. When I got to the part about Stan leaving his fingerprints behind and now lying low, like some fugitive with a gripe and a gun, Dean interrupted me.

"It's a TV! He's acting like this is some heist!" I imagined a diamond shimmering in a display case and Stan emerging from the shadows dressed in black, grabbing the jewel.

"What's with the fingerprints?" Dean exclaimed. "He never heard of gloves?" Kelvin let out a percussive laugh, shaking his head side to side as Dean continued, "He should just turn himself in. Get it over with!" Kelvin mumbled *You right, man, you right* before squinting and tilting his head into a question. He could see both sides. Both sides had a point.

The producer tapped the glass. Kelvin took his place at the table and adjusted the mic. I followed Dean into the sound booth. The producer's computer screen showed a green pulse of sound waves swelling and cresting and falling and swelling. I went into a waking daydream. Then the lights and Kelvin's voice stopped. The producer swiveled on his high stool to face me.

"Isn't there one more guy to record today?" he asked. I didn't want to lie. But I didn't want to tell the truth. I felt trapped between truths. There was the truth of the crime. The truth of Stan's addiction. And the truth about writing your way out of crimes that can lead to prison. That last truth was the one that had brought us together. That was the story I was expecting to hear today.

"Something came up," I said.

"Okay," the producer said. But it was not okay. This was supposed to be a good day, a victory lap, an audiobook coming out of our book that already had a great following. The icing on the cake. Instead, it felt like tears at my birthday party.

Sit at the piano. Put your thumb on middle C, your pointer finger on E, and your middle finger on G. You have just played a C major chord. This is the chord you land on in "Happy Birthday" when you say the person's name. Clean, elemental, happy. Nobody puts their pinky finger on the B, a half step away from the high C. No one plays a C major seven. That's too much dissonance. Too much tension. On other occasions, with other music, dissonance is key. Tension can make music interesting. But tension is the last thing you want on a birthday.

It was not okay that Stan stole a TV. I could not rationalize, minimize, rename, or subordinate the belief I had that it was wrong to go into someone's home, take something from the exact spot where they'd left it, and, in this way, disturb their basic expectation of returning home unperturbed. It was not okay that he did not seem to care about the people he violated. He was not remorseful but defiant. It was C major seven all the way home from the studio.

A few days later, Stan came to the office. When I saw him in the door frame, though, I did not see the man I usually saw grinning, dapping me up, and rapping *What's happening?* I saw a cowboy after a long ride. Dust in his beard. Horse tied up, watering, but ready to run with a whistle. He sat and splayed his legs. He knew I would have more questions like the ones I'd asked over the phone. He wasn't in the mood but had resigned himself to it.

I asked again about the dude with no name. He again insisted that the dude was the mastermind, the one the police should be searching for. I was beginning to doubt there was a dude. I asked again if he'd been high that night or planning to get high and, if so, on what substance. But like a stranger in a saloon dealing three-card monte, he dazzled with verbal sleight of hand. By the time he was done shuffling my questions about the past into his concerns about the present, I could not tell which card was the lady.

"It's a long shot," he mused, opening up a new topic. "It's possible the couple won't press charges. Maybe they already decided. Or they could be persuaded." He leaned forward and flexed his brow. "The question is, how do we get to them?"

"Wait, what?"

"They'll listen to you, Dave. They're a young couple. White folks. Professionals like you."

"You want me to *talk* to these people?"

"Just an introduction. Tell them how you know me. Tell them who I am. Say just enough so that they'll hear me out."

"I'm not trying to host a sit-down with your victims, Stan."

"I want to apologize. I want to make amends. It was a violation. And that was wrong." It sounded like he was feeling some remorse. I felt a clarifying breeze. A letter! I could help him write a letter! If he were writing and I were coaching, I would be on the sidelines where I wanted to be, instead of on the field playing.

He talked. I typed. With his record, he said, there would be little chance for leniency in court. If they wanted to bury him, he understood. But he hoped they would consider giving him a chance to resolve the matter outside of court. I printed the letter, put it into an envelope, and handed it to him. He handed me a scrap of paper. It was the address. He wanted me to deliver it.

"No."

"Dave, let me explain something to you."

"No."

"I am a Black man in Virginia with a criminal record. If they send me back to court, the judge will not see the man you know. The judge will just see a felon. And the judgment will be prison." He held my gaze. He was completely still. This is how it came to be that Stan left the office without the letter, and I drove past the Confederate statues and stately homes on Monument Avenue, looking for the one he stole from.

I told myself that delivering the letter was a way of keeping a Black man out of prison. It was enabling him to come clean and apologize. He was offering to bring back the TV or pay restitution. He was telling the story his way while avoiding the more punitive and limiting story that he would be forced to hear in court. I subordinated my concerns about his reasons for stealing the TV to the bigger reasoning in my head about justice. Treating addiction with prison was wrong. There would be time later for confronting him about the crack and the lying, and the stealing. That time would come. But not now.

I parked the car. It was eerily quiet. I could hear the leaves in the breeze. The apartment building was set back from the sidewalk. A three-story fortress of tan brick and white balustrades overlooking a patchy green lawn. I stood on the sidewalk at the periphery of the property. I imagined the couple inside doing whatever. I took a few steps down the path toward the front door. Then I froze. Would they hear me opening the door to the vestibule? Would they go down and check their mail, find the letter, read it right then, and see me walking away? Would they come calling after me? The letter was unsigned. Would they think that I wrote it?

I walked away, feigning a nonchalance I was not feeling. In the car, I exhaled, calmed my heart, and considered the situation again. I probably could have delivered the letter. I didn't even know if the couple was home. And even if they were, how likely is it that they would have come down the stairs to check their mail right then? It wasn't rational. But if they somehow intercepted me and demanded an explanation, I would not be able to amplify what was in the letter and ask them to meet Stan so that he could return the TV and apologize. I would not be able to defend his breaking and entering and stealing. If they freaked out and called the police, I would freak out harder, unable to figure out if I should be more afraid or embarrassed.

I returned to my office, taped the letter to the door, and called Stan. I told him that I could not go through with it. If he wanted to do it, the letter was on the door. We met in the office a few days later, after he called to tell me he had delivered the letter. I asked him how it went.

"I knocked gently, right? Then I took two steps back, to show deference."

"Right."

"When the lady answered, I took a step in and handed her the letter. Then I stepped back and clasped my hands out front where she could see them. When she finished reading it, she looked up." He dropped his voice to a whisper as he re-created the next part of the story.

"I told her, right, 'I'm sorry.'" He bowed his head. "*'I'm really sorry.'*"

"What did she say?"

"Nothing."

"What was her face saying?"

"She was shocked. She closed the door. I heard it lock."

"Sounds like you scared her."

"Maybe." He sighed as he shifted in his seat. "But they dropped the charges."

"What?"

"I looked it up this morning before I came here." I couldn't believe it. He had kept the case out of court after all!

"What about the TV?"

"No one wanted it. Not the couple. Not the detectives."

"So, what did you do with it?"

"That thing was more trouble than it was worth. I put it out in the trash." And that was that. He did not gloat. But he did not seem chastened. He was just ready to move on. I could not.

No one goes looking for cognitive dissonance. No one wants to feel the discomfort of a contradiction. To study the phenomenon, researchers will often lie to subjects about the nature of the experiment. One researcher told the subjects—college students at Iowa State University in 1967—that they were going to rate the persuasiveness of speeches. They were told that the speeches had been made imperfectly with portable tape recorders. To reduce the static and hear the message better, they could press a button. But the researchers lied. The tapes were not imperfectly made. Crackly static had been added on purpose. The real goal was not to judge the persuasiveness of the speeches but to find out when and why a subject pressed the button to clarify the message and when they left that button alone.

There was a speech that maligned Christianity as evil, a speech that affirmed the link between smoking and lung cancer, and a speech that disputed that link. Between these main speeches, there were filler speeches about chewing gum and choosing classes that were not part of the experiment proper but a part of the misdirection. To figure out why the subjects pressed the buttons during the Christianity speech and the smoking speeches, researchers surveyed the subjects ahead of time to figure out which ones were religious and which ones smoked. Christians who reported a high level of church attendance and praying made no effort to hear the speech accusing Christianity of evildoing. But those with weaker ties to Christianity pressed that button. Smokers pressed the button when they heard the message disputing the link to cancer, which at that time still seemed up for debate. They did not press the button when the speech confirmed the link to cancer.[37]

The students in this study had not come to the lab to get their beliefs rattled. But they knew that they were entering a lab. At some level, they knew that they were going to be tested.

The Sound of Music Studio where we were recording the audiobook was not a psychology lab. Neither was my office in the English Department at VCU. These were not places set up by researchers conducting experiments on cognitive dissonance, unless of course that researcher was me—unless I was the one lying to myself by setting up a multiyear experiment that I told myself was about the possibility of writing your way out of the cycle of crime and incarceration, but was really an experiment on the morality of crime.

This is the story Stan later told me. It was 2 a.m. when he got out of the bar and discovered that his car was missing. It could have been towed. It had a lapsed inspection. It could have been stolen. It didn't matter now. Everything he owned was in that car. He slept in it when he could not afford to pay the rent. He was going to sleep in it that night. Now he had nowhere to go and no money for a motel.

He hated that he was always running low on money. He hated Thrasher, his boss at The Local. Thrasher kept reneging on raises and bonuses while telling him how lucky he was to have a job with a shift meal and a shift drink. Stan always kept the back door to the restaurant rigged so that he could get in if he needed to. The cash register would be a different story. He would have to bend some metal for that.

He wore a garbage bag over his head. He came through the alley, opened the back door, and left with eighteen dollars. The police identified him from the surveillance video. There was a warrant out for his arrest . . . again. Again, he asked me to intercede. He wanted to keep the case out of court.

Unlike the couple I had never met, I had met Thrasher in passing when I visited Stan at The Local. I felt I could reason with him. He remembered meeting me when I called. He knew who I was and that Stan had written his life story with me. But he could not let a break-in go unpunished. Had he not given Stan a chance with this job? Was this burglary not the opposite of gratitude? What kind of example would it set for the other employees if he just let the matter pass? I had not thought of any of this and was honestly persuaded. And so, when he insisted that we just let the courts handle the case, I had no stomach to argue otherwise.

I did not go to court. A phone call to Thrasher was one thing. But showing up in court and showing my face was something else. Stan told me in a letter from jail that Thrasher was livid that day in court. It was not just his property but his livelihood that had been violated. He argued strenuously for the strongest possible punishment. In his letter, Stan asked me to assemble clippings about the book and our events so that he could prove to the court that he was more than this one incident, that he'd had a positive impact in the community, too.

I went to bed angry. In my dream, I was walking with Stan on a breezy boardwalk in some resort town. We got separated. I don't know how or why. I think I stopped to tie my shoe. When I looked up, Stan was gone. I heard a woman screaming. I ran to help her. When I arrived, she told me that someone had stolen her purse. She was shaken. I let her use my phone. I waited with her until her friend arrived. Together, they called the police.

"After they left, I saw you," I told Stan in my letter. "You were off the boardwalk behind two buildings, waving me over. You had her purse. You were counting the money. You offered me half for doing my part. I said Look, I am your teacher. I am your friend. But I am not your soldier."

I never sent him any clippings about the book. Stan wrote back acknowledging that I had a right to be angry. He thanked me for my insightful dream. The damage to The Local was too small to warrant prison time or even an insurance payout.

Stan did his time in the new city jail. Unlike the old jail where we had the class and where he lived on a tier with over a hundred men and no privacy or air conditioning all through the summer, here you got your own air-conditioned cell. I knew about these cells. Before the new jail was filled with prisoners, we volunteers were invited to tour it. To get from one section to another, you waited while a deputy watched your image on a screen and pressed a button to let you through. Gone were the clanking skeleton keys and grimy linoleum. This place was hospital-clean. The hallways were white and grey, neutral, bureaucratic.

The day room of the pod was shiny and shadowless. The white walls were broken up by a thin, matte yellow railing connecting the first and second floors. Our tour guide led us to the door of an open cell on the first floor. One of the volunteers strode into the cell, spreading her arms wide, basking in the glint of natural light coming from the glass block windows.

"This is nice!" she enthused, like we were at an open house, like there were cookies baking in an oven nearby, fresh flowers in a vase, brochures on the table. I fell back as the others queued up for their turn in captivity. When they finished, I slipped into the cell and stifled a sob.

Stan got out after several months. We caught up over the phone.

"What was it like being back in?"

"I went to the quartermaster. You know, receiving."

"Right."

"They assign you a cell."

"Uh-huh."

"And I lucked out, man. No cellie!"

"That's good."

"Yeah, but when I got there?" He hesitated. "When I walked in there, right? I was not alone."

"They lied?"

"No, they told the truth. But I was not alone." Was someone squatting in his cell? Was there a deputy in there to mess with him?

"There was a copy of *Writing Our Way Out* in there."

"No!"

"There I was on the back cover, smiling. I remember the day we took that picture in the old jail."

"In the chapel, yeah."

"That was a good day."

I felt the corners of my mouth pinching into a smile. I remembered not just that day, but all the days and weeks and months that we spent in that space together, writing, building, becoming. I heard C major. Clean, elemental, happy.

26
Presentence Report

Stan

After you're found guilty by a judge or a jury of your so-called peers, the guilty verdict then accelerates like an out-of-control eighteen-wheeler coursing down the highway. The next phase is called a presentence report. This is when the court gathers all of the facts that have been filed against you so that they can determine your sentence, ranging from one day of incarceration all the way up to execution, if your state allows that. Once presentencing has been done, the judge has all the information they need to slaughter and hang you on the judicial tree. It's a new way to hang a brother, or, better yet, those who are low-income, who lack strong representation. Cash and prominence will always change the trajectory of one's sentence.

What I write today is not some judicial evaluation of myself. A court-ordered presentence report is about cold facts. My presentence report is the truth. Truthfully, I have devoted far too much time to my lower vibration, being street-minded. Yes, I take full responsibility and accountability for my actions, past and present. But there were some mitigating factors. Those are my truths.

In 2015, I was released back into free society in Richmond, Virginia. My heart was in the right place, meaning I had every intention to be a law-abiding citizen and productive member of my community. And I was, for a season or two. I had a job at The Local, an Irish bar by the VCU campus. The boss was a big man named Thrasher. I saw how he handled other people abruptly. How he handled the waitresses and bartenders. How he belittled me in ways he thinks I didn't recognize. But I needed the job. After work one night, I went out to relax. I stayed out late. When I got back, I discovered that my car had been towed from where I had parked it at work. Everything I owned was in that car. Everything. I was angry! How could I rectify this?

My lower vibration showed up. I went into autopilot. I wasn't just angry about the car but about the whole situation with the job. And now I needed money to get my car. I am a predator in my lower vibration. Fuck Thrasher! He acts like he's all this? What I'm gonna do is show him that he ain't all this! I'm gonna take from him. I'm on the hunt.

Now, that's not even a rational thought. It comes from my time in the Department of Corrections. When I met a bully in prison, I couldn't help but fuck with him. I just couldn't help but un-throne his ass. Thrasher was a bully. Six-foot-something, four hundred pounds. Acted like he was a tough guy. I had to challenge that.

Stealing from The Local didn't give me the outcome I wanted. Not just because I only walked away with eighteen dollars. Not just because I got caught. But because I care about being a productive citizen. That matters to me. The truth is that you can't take a step forward and a step backward at the same time. How far had I really come in my resocialization?

I had to stop committing crimes. It wasn't the doing time that bothered me. Incarceration couldn't hurt me anymore. What bothered me was my son. My son told me that if I was going to have a relationship with him, I had to be free. It also bothered me that these crimes put my friendship with Dave in jeopardy. So, I had to let go of my criminal mindset. I knew that.

Now, a criminal mindset and drug use are two different things. You can be a hippie and do drugs and eat dandelions and all that and never commit a crime. When I was living on Hanes Avenue and getting high, I never committed a crime against another person. I committed crimes against myself. But I never went out and took from nobody so I could get high.

I have never lived in a neighborhood that didn't normalize drugs. That's low income. It's understandable. You want to feel better? Take this. You didn't get a job? No problem. Take this. The only thing I was unwilling to do was sell it. I always thought that was going to exacerbate the problem. I've spent far too much time swimming in saltwater, negative environments. It's natural to me. But I don't become a predator there.

I'm an isolated person anyway. You're not going to know a whole lot about me. You're only going to know what I present to you. I always present the truth, but I don't give you all the details. I show you a picture where something is wrong, but it's up to you to find it. If you don't get it, you don't get it. It's the same thing in jail. You don't come out of your cell saying, God dammit, I'm homesick! You don't go around showing everyone where you're fractured, hurt. When the parole board turns you down, you don't cry. You say, I'm okay. But really, you're not okay.

My father died when I was in prison. And I couldn't go to the funeral. I didn't have a chance to sit in a room where he was at peace. Now, how the hell am I supposed to have peace? Who taught me how to have peace? Nobody.

When my father adopted me as a baby, I was a sick child. At the hospital, I couldn't breathe easily outside of my oxygen tent. I asked him once, *Why did you pick me? You could have picked a baby whose chest was crying.* I couldn't cry. I couldn't breathe. But he did pick me. I know that my father loved me. He did a lot for me. He taught me how to take care of myself. But he didn't like me. And I get that. That's why he abandoned me to live in that one-bedroom on Grace Street when I didn't turn out like he wanted. You can love your child, but not the shit that your child does. I understand that now. Still, my father was a significant—a pinnacle—part of my life. I wish I could be in his presence again.

My mother died when I was in prison, too. Once again, I couldn't go to the funeral. My sisters felt that I didn't need to be there. But I did need to be there. I wanted to be present in the reality of it. Not sitting on the sidelines, watching. I didn't have a chance to grieve. They didn't even send me an obituary.

Today, I wish I could hear my mother say one more time, *You're going to be all right*. That's the most difficult thing about this time, coming out into society without a mother or a father. It feels overwhelming to go forward when I can't release myself from my past.

It's been a struggle. I've been struggling my whole life, just like I started out as a baby, struggling to breathe, to live, to exist. One battle after another. How long can I do it? In resocialization, they teach you how to tie a tie, where to go get soup, and how to take advantage of this benefit or that benefit. But they don't really deal with the true person inside. They don't help you develop who you need to be or figure out who your authentic self is, because they never really ask. They just go by your presentence report. What you have done. They never ask why you did it.

27
Mercy

Dave

The closer we get to mass incarceration and extreme levels of punishment, the more I believe it's necessary to recognize that we all need mercy, we all need justice, and—perhaps—we all need some measure of unmerited grace.
—Bryan Stevenson, *Just Mercy: A Story of Justice and Redemption*[38]

Spring, 2018. The basketball nets had been raised. Rows of seating had been arranged. An enormous podium dominated the stage. Soon, lawyer and author Bryan Stevenson would be behind it to share his story of defending people in the worst prisons in America. I had never been in the VIP club in VCU's Siegel Center overlooking the basketball court before. But I knew that this club was typically filled with patrons of VCU basketball, politicians, journalists, and celebrities. That night, it was filled with people who had been to prison and those who advocate for them. That night, the curated party included Dean, Terence, Kelvin, and Stan sipping sweet tea and eating hors d'oeuvres.

The club had the décor of a mid-level hotel. Bright pendant lights, brick walls, and taupe armchairs near long black tables and barstools to perch on. Mike Herring, Richmond's commonwealth's attorney, was in the middle of the room by himself with a bottle of water. In his white button-down shirt and dark slacks, he looked like a candidate at a town hall event. A young Obama. He had the same-shaped head. That same lean frame. I had heard him speak at a criminal justice reform event a few years ago, and I was surprised to hear him complain about how many cases his office had to prosecute. He understood that his job was to uphold the law, but he was skeptical that prosecuting and incarcerating so many people would improve public safety.

It hit me then that his office was the one that incarcerated the guys standing next to me. He may even have been the one who did it. I decided that I wanted to meet him and made my way over to introduce myself. I shook his hand and began telling him my story of teaching writing at the jail.

"They wrote their ways out," I said, gesturing to the guys, who by now had formed a semicircle around us. "But ultimately, I don't think they should have been in." A server in a black vest and tuxedo shirt approached with a platter of mushroom caps. I filled my tiny plate. "It's something I've noticed over the years teaching there. Most of the people I meet just don't seem to belong there." I paused for an objection or qualification. None were made. "They need a consequence, I understand. But jail . . ." I trailed off. Then I heard myself asking a question. It came out before I realized what I was truly asking.

"Mike, can you imagine sending fewer people to jail?"

Had he actually been a candidate at a town-hall event, this would have been the moment when he eased off the high stool and took a few steps toward me, microphone in hand. He lifted his water bottle and took a quick sip.

"What did you have in mind?"

"I was just thinking: Why do I have to go to the jail to teach? Why not do the same class—"

"Here?" He pointed to the faux wood floor of the club. "You would do that *here?*" I couldn't believe it either! I hadn't come to the VIP club to pitch a program. But I couldn't have planned a better pitch. I'd just named a problem, given my credentials for addressing it, and yielded the floor to my coauthors, who were now giving testimonials. I ate one mushroom cap after another.

When the last man had finished sharing his experience of the class, Mike urged me to call him on Monday morning. After he left, I wondered why, in all my years of going to the jail to teach writing, I had never imagined looking up the man who sends people there. Justice was not faceless. It was Mike's face, and Mike was listening to me. Why had I envisioned a criminal justice system like some machine hiding its cogs?

In a 1969 task force report to the federal government about the root causes of crime, Daniel Freed argued that the "criminal justice system" is really more of a nonsystem: "A system implies some unity of purpose and organized interrelationship among component parts." The reality is an uncoordinated set of agencies—police, courts, corrections—that more often than not regard each other with skepticism or hostility.[39] The police have already decided that the person they arrested is guilty. Some judges and defense attorneys suspect the police violated the law to make their arrests. Attorneys and judges are not prone to agree on the facts of the case anyway. Few judges have actually been inside a prison, and many see them as failed institutions.

The skepticism and lack of coordination in these roles are magnified at the macro level. Cities, towns, and states run their own police departments, courts, jails, and prisons. All compete for tax dollars set aside for "law enforcement." Without a central administrative structure to fund these agencies and facilitate communication between them, there is no way to know if "the system" is working. It works if each agency fulfills its mission: for the police, arrests; for the courts, convictions; for the jails and prisons, incarceration. On top of all this is the federal prison system with its own agents, attorneys, courts, and prisons.

Freed wrote his report in 1969, standing at the base of the mountain of a national prison population that was about three hundred thousand people. By the time he died in 2010,[40] the prison population had formed a wintry peak of over 2.2 million people, with an excessive percentage of them Black and brown.[41] The big picture horror of these numbers and demographics overshadows the mundanity of it. Politics may have spurred the "tough on crime" movement that built mass incarceration. But the non-system of administrators, lawyers, politicians, police, and judges made it routine.

The party in the VIP club pulsed on. Dean nudged me and pointed. A crowd had formed across the room. Bryan Stevenson had just come through the door and was walking slowly, taking selfies and shaking hands. After mingling, he followed Shelli, the host for the event, through the crowd and toward a side room, a club within the club. I had never seen this inner sanctum, but I knew it existed. I knew about this stop on his itinerary, too. I had been waiting for it, actually. This was the place where Stevenson would meet privately with people who had been to prison.

"What's the plan, Dave?" Stan asked. I could tell his adrenaline was pulsing. He was becoming the salesman he used to be, selling magazines door-to-door all those years ago as a young man. He was dressed for the part in black leather shoes, light grey slacks, and a matching jacket over a pin-striped shirt. His hair was short and lightly greased. His face was clean-shaven. Ever since he got out of jail a few months ago, he had been hungry for a fresh start.

"I think you should start," he said. "You're the professor. I'm your closer. The last voice he hears." I nodded. I could see him strategizing for the sale.

"All right," I began. The men huddled up around me. "We won't have much time. When we get in there, I'll tell the story of the class. Just enough to set it up so you can share some of your stories." I turned to Stan. "When the last man is done speaking, give Stevenson the book. Tell him we want to help more people write their ways out. Ask him to hold it up and mention it in his speech."

"I got you," Stan said. I gave him a copy of *Writing Our Way Out*. He held it flat against his chest like a Bible. Then he stepped away, gathering his thoughts. I stared through the long, rectangular window down at the court. The chairs on the floor were packed. The stands, too. Thousands of people could learn about our book tonight, possibly accomplishing more in one moment than I had accomplished in a year's worth of book events, social media posts, interviews in the local press, and classes.

Shelli, the host, emerged from the inner sanctum and invited people who had been incarcerated to meet the man inside. Instinctively, I followed Dean and the others but was detained. Gently but firmly, she reminded me that this was a time set aside for people who had been to prison. I was so accustomed to walking into rooms with the guys that I must have blocked out the obvious. I apologized and watched with longing as they slipped away. Ten minutes later, they reappeared.

"How did it go?" I asked. Terence let out a barking laugh. Kelvin shook his head in awe.

"Stan had his talk game on, Dave," Kelvin said.

"For real," Dean added. Stan looked like the cat who got the cream. I gave him a curious smile and nodded my head for him to tell the story.

"Okay, so, I explained the class, right? I told him how you set it up to follow the drama on the internal. Not the external of who we appear to be."

"Right."

"Then I held up the book, and I told him, 'This is our lives, man. *Our lives!*'" He held the word until his breath ran out, locking our attention with an intense gaze. Even the guys who had already heard the story were listening closely, like they were hearing it for the first time. "Dave, I believe his spirit heard what I was saying."

I nodded. I mean, how could he not? I was hearing it now.

"'Then I told him, 'Hey, listen man, we're just trying to change the narrative, like you're doing.' Then I gave him the book and asked him to hold it up on stage."

"Good."

"But check it out. He said no! He said he doesn't even bring his own book up to the podium. No papers. Nothing. He doesn't want the distraction of anything in his hands. So, I was like Cool. I understand. Can you give the people our title? And Dave! He balked!" Stan pushed off from the spot where he was standing, threw his arms up in disbelief, turned around fast, walked away, then pivoted back just as abruptly. When he returned to our huddle, his shoulders were pressed up against the seams of his jacket like an athlete who'd stepped straight out of the weight room and into a suit.

"So, I had to break it down for him. I said, 'Man, you're in a basketball stadium! You've come here from out of town. You're the visiting team. We're the home team. Show the audience you know the home team!'"

"Oh, that's awesome!"

"I know how to close," Stan said, as much to himself as to us.

A bell rang, signaling to us that the speech was about to begin. We filed out the door and down the stairs. Our seats in the front row had been reserved.

Shelli introduced Stevenson's work with the Equal Justice Initiative, representing people suffering on death row, in solitary confinement, who had been wrongfully convicted, who suffered from mental health problems, the list went on and on. He rose to acknowledge his accolades. Terence let out a "WOOT-WOOT!" like we were at a real basketball game. Stevenson smiled and waved to the crowd. Then he thanked everyone who had brought him to Richmond, pausing to reflect on the people with whom he'd had thoughtful conversations throughout the day.

"Just now, before I got out here, I met a group of formerly imprisoned men who wrote a book about their lives with a professor here at this university. Maybe you've heard of it?" Kelvin elbowed me in the ribs. Stan leaned in, arms on his knees like a coach concentrating on an important play. "It's called *Writing My Wrongs*."

Stan scraped his chair back hard and lolled his head side to side. His face was a mix of *motherfucker!* and *whatever*. A moment later, he got up and walked out amidst a trickle of applause for Shaka Senghor's excellent prison memoir.

In the morning, as I prepared to call Mike, the commonwealth's attorney, I wondered about the logistics of diverting people from a jail sentence to my memoir writing course. The course, Writing and Social Change, already appeared in the university bulletin. I had been teaching it in the Open Minds program at the jail for seven years. College students could take it for credit. People in jail could take it for free. If I offered that same course on campus instead of at the jail, nothing would change except the location. College students would still take it for credit. The people diverted from the court would take it for free. Just like with Open Minds, the course in this new program would be a regular part of my teaching load, so my time would be covered. From the point of view of the university and the Richmond Commonwealth Attorney's Office, the program would be free.

I explained the plan to Mike. He liked it and wanted to meet on campus to flesh out the details. He wanted the guys to be there—whichever ones wanted to participate. Instinctively, I wanted them all there, but since this would be a small class of ten college students and ten people diverted from court, and I wanted to find a way to pay the guys like teaching assistants, I could not include more than a few at one time. I consoled myself with the bigger vision that, if we did the class regularly, I could rotate the guys in and out as coaches.

I invited Stan and Dean to the meeting. Mike explained to us the criteria that he would use to choose low-level offenders. No violent crimes. No sex crimes. No possession of illegal substances with the intent to distribute. It was common sense. We did not want to increase the risks to public safety. He went on to elaborate that the people he selected would be offered a plea bargain to join the program. So long as they fulfilled the course requirements—the writing assignments, presentations, and attendance—they would get their charges vacated. No jail time. No criminal record.

He spoke directly and simply. He was refreshingly not an academic. And so, when he leaned back and folded his arms behind his head, all I could see was the rationality of the plan. When I matched it with my plan, it felt as if I were trying on a new pair of gloves. I stretched my fingers. It felt good. I made a fist and relaxed. It still felt good. But as the meetings piled up over the next few months, I began to wonder. Could I shake hands with Mike to close this deal?

I decided to get some advice from Cathy, the VCU administrator who had helped me create Open Minds. She listened attentively as I explained the idea. Then she explained it back to me. What I was proposing was a contract between the university and the Richmond Commonwealth Attorney's Office. Tactfully, she elaborated that I did not have the authority to create a contract obligating the university to provide services to another institution, possibly incurring risk and liability.

"What risk?"

"Some people might be wary of bringing people convicted of crimes to campus."

"Oh."

"University Counsel would need to write an MOU." I wrinkled my nose. "A memorandum of understanding," she said. "A contract that would authorize the partnership and describe everyone's roles and responsibilities. Both parties would then need to sign off on it."

She advised me to write up the proposal and share it with an attorney that she recommended in University Counsel. I drafted the proposal, got Mike's input, and emailed it to the attorney. A week later, I located the office that I'd never known existed in the twelve years I'd been working at the university, buzzed the intercom to the front door, explained my business to the disembodied voice, gained entry, and walked down to the last office at the end of the hall.

Sarah, the attorney Cathy told me to contact, greeted me from behind her desk, a printed copy of my proposal in front of her. The sleeve of her blazer brushed the paper as she underlined and made notes. She lifted her head to address me and invited me to sit. Her steady bearing suggested that she was accustomed to meetings like this.

"It says that the Commonwealth Attorney's Office will send people diverted from court to your class, correct?" I nodded, wondering why she needed to confirm that fact. Suddenly, I was wary of facts. She underlined the word class. "And VCU students will be in this class, as well?" I narrowed my eyes and nodded. "University policy does not allow nonstudents to be in a classroom with students."

I stared in shock. The meeting had just begun, and already, we were at an impasse. The program was the class. The class was the program. If I could not have "nonstudents" in my writing class, I would not be able to have a program.

"I'll need to talk to my lawyer. I mean, Mike. I'll need to ask Mike about that," I said, registering this bizarre new add-on to my professor job: Mediating between the legal departments of two large state institutions.

"She is correct," Mike told me over the phone. "They are not students. But she is also incorrect. They are not nonstudents." I waited to hear the rest of his reasoning. There had to be more.

"I know you think of them as your students, but technically, they're not."

"But that's a problem. If we can't have—"

"They are *diverted participants,*" he interrupted. A sly smile spread across my face. The definitional move! "Tell her that we will not have nonstudents in a class with students. We will have diverted participants fulfilling the obligations of a program approved by university administration."

I returned to University Counsel the next week, buzzed the intercom to get in, and tried to repress a jaunty stride down the long hall to Sarah's office. When I got there, I was actually grinning, so she grinned, reflexively, then invited me to sit. I remained standing. I only had a few lines to recite, but I was going to deliver them with conviction.

"Mike said you're right. We won't have nonstudents in a class with students. We will have diverted participants fulfilling a program approved by university administration." Her smile shifted into that flat affect I knew from the last meeting. I sat down now, thrilled by the silence that I had created, but she just wiped a stray hair from her forehead and uncapped her felt pen. Like a chess master conceding the loss of her knight while eyeing my rook, she crossed off "nonstudent" and changed it to "diverted participant." Then she circled the word criminal in the title of the proposal, "A Criminal Justice Diversion Program." I felt a wave of logic coming. I braced for impact.

"The diverted participants could impact campus security."

"How do you know?"

"They have been convicted of crimes."

"Low-level offenses."

"Still, crimes."

"Crimes that the commonwealth's attorney believes will not threaten public safety."

"According to his office, yes, but it is possible his risk assessment is different from ours."

"Who decides our risk assessment?"

"In this case, VCU Police. You should run this by Chief Venuti. He may want to post officers outside of the classroom."

My eyes widened. It was true that when I taught the class at the jail, officers would walk by the classroom. But they were never in the classroom or posted specifically to monitor us. Was she saying that in order to prevent people from going to jail, I would need to make the campus more like a jail?

I took my case to the chief of campus police. John Venuti greeted me in the lobby of the police station like an old friend. He had a starched white shirt, black tie, gold badge, and a trim, wide moustache. His eyes pinched at the corners when he smiled. I heard an Italian accent. New York Italian. An echo of my family. I began to think of him as that uncle I see a few times a year with the gold chain and the hairy chest who slaps me on the back and says, *How YOU doing?*

We walked back to his office and settled in. I told him my story of teaching writing at the jail to help people get some control over their lives. I went on to explain how that led to Open Minds, where we bring VCU students into the jail for classes with the residents. Then I told him that I was now interested in teaching my life-writing class on campus with VCU students and low-level offenders diverted from court. He nodded generously when I mentioned Mike Herring.

"So, what can I do for you?" he asked, spreading his arms.

"University Counsel told me to come talk to you." He shrugged like, so? "They want your risk assessment. They thought maybe you would want to increase patrols in that area when class is in session or post officers outside the door." He winced like someone was trying to tell him when to flip *his* burgers on *his* grill. Then he leaned back in his leather chair and folded his arms behind his neck, just relaxing back there between the American flag and the flag of Virginia. He waited for me to say more. I searched for a voice, a disposition, that could match his posture. I thought of my uncle Sal. Then I leaned in.

"Are you worried, John?"

He smiled that smile. I continued.

"Are you *worried* at all about low-level offenders *hand-picked* by our commonwealth's attorney, taking a class with VCU students? The *same class* that I have been teaching for years at our city jail?" The smile became a chuckle. He slid forward on the wheels of his chair. He'd decided something.

"Oh, no. Not at all. In fact—" He opened a drawer, pulled out a piece of paper, and held it up. "Could you take these people, too?" It was a list of VCU students. He paraphrased their charges—DUI, possession of a controlled substance, shoplifting, and simple assault. We spent the rest of our meeting seriously entertaining the possibility of getting those students into my class instead of doing the community service hours he was going to give them.

I left his office feeling like I had just had coffee and cannoli with The Man. I was sated yet energized. He did not want to post officers outside my classroom to protect VCU students from low-level offenders. He wanted to fill that classroom with VCU students convicted of similar, low-level offenses. I trotted back to the Office of University Counsel like a homerun slugger. But when I shared my joy with Sarah, she just shrugged, uncapped her felt pen, and checked off "risk assessment" from her list. Why wasn't she upset? She should be upset. I was two for three now.

"You understand I'm just trying to advise you in this process?" I did not. "My job is to work through these scenarios so that all parties can make an informed decision. I don't have any stake in the outcome." Apparently, I had misread her flat expression as poker face. It was no such thing. She was not speaking for herself but for the bureaucracy she was charged with executing.

As Max Weber explains it, "bureaucracy strives everywhere for the creation of a 'right to the office.'" It does not secure that right by force of personality but by "domination through *knowledge*. This is the feature of it which makes it specifically rational." This is also what makes it impersonal, which is how I was experiencing it. Bureaucracy functions through "calculable rules" that exist "without regard to persons." The rules exist to justify the authority of the one whose office is charged with enforcing them. Before any decision is made, there is always a "weighing of ends and means."[42]

The question then becomes: Who sets the scales? Who determines what is to be weighed and measured? I wanted to see fewer people in jail. It seemed commonsensical and merciful. But as Malcom Bull observes, "The modern theory of the state, like the modern theory of justice, develops alongside, and to some degree depends on, the repudiation of mercy."[43] To the modern sensibility, mercy can seem whimsical, a departure from precedent and rules.

Who, then, is responsible for offering mercy? The university is not set up to help people avoid jail. But that does not mean it cannot serve that function. It can depart from the precedent and rules. Claudia Card reasons that "if some offenders deserve punishment, it seems that some of them also deserve mercy."[44] Mercy, according to Card, is for people who would suffer more than is warranted given their basic character, and in light of their "peculiar misfortunes." Mercy is not a part of the law. It is an escape hatch from the law.

"Who makes the final decision?" I asked Sarah.

"It resolves with a memorandum of understanding that we create, which is then signed by the provost and the commonwealth's attorney."

"Why the provost?"

"She is the chief academic officer. You're proposing a change to the curriculum."

"The course is already in the curriculum. I have been teaching it at the jail for years as part of the Open Minds program."

"But now you are proposing to teach it here in the . . ." She looks down at her notes. "In the *Write Your Way Out: Criminal Justice Diversion Program*. The provost approves new programs after they make it through the curriculum committee."

My chest tightened. I knew about that committee. If she sent my proposal there, someone could take it hostage, tying it up in a dark subset of policy before demanding a ransom that I could not afford. The program could die in that committee. More people would go to jail. When I spoke again, the words came out louder and faster than before.

"We do not need the curriculum committee to review a course that already exists in the curriculum. The participants who have taken the class at the jail are similar to the ones that the CA's Office would divert to campus."

"But you would still need—"

"The approval of the dean should be sufficient. The dean oversees the English Department. The dean approved the program at the jail. The dean reports to the provost. The dean could be the signee for the provost."

She shrugged. As she told me—she had no stake in the outcome. The final MOU was prepared with two signature lines: one for the commonwealth's attorney and one for the dean.

Before we could begin the program in January of 2018, though, Stan got into an argument with his girlfriend and took it out on his car, which was registered to her name because he could not afford registration or insurance. This meant a new charge, a new conviction, and incarceration in Henrico, where the incident took place. Now I had to tell Mike that Stan could not participate as a program coach because of this new charge.

I was embarrassed to share this news, but Mike took it in stride. The goal was to divert people away from court without increasing any risk to public safety. Stan's charge had not created a threat to public safety. In fact, had his case been in Richmond, he might have been a good candidate for the program. I pulled Kelvin in from the bench to take his place. He and Dean became the program coaches, the ones who had been through the class, who would help the diverted participants make it through.

* * *

"Look at all these women coming to see all these knuckleheads," Terence muttered as we made our way toward the receptionist's desk for visiting hours at the jail. I turned to him with a questioning face. "I can say it now," he explained. "I'm not the one locked up."

I laughed. We filled out our forms, dropped some money into Dean's account, and found him on the other side of the glass. His expression sagged like a Mylar balloon three days after the party. He had a nosebleed. He kept adjusting a spiral of tissue paper he had fashioned to stop the drip.

It was April. He had made it through most of the class as one of the coaches. Then he got arrested in a motel with a cache of marijuana. His girlfriend called me the night after the arrest to let me know.

There was only one stool. Terence sat down first and released a stream of optimism tempered with realism at Dean. *God has a plan for you. The commonwealth has another one. Keep your head up. Keep your eyes open.* Dean listened, nodding in slow motion. They had not always seen eye to eye on the outside. But in here they could see each other clearly. Then Terence and I switched positions.

"I'm sorry, Dave. I know you're disappointed. I'm disappointed, too."

"Why didn't you talk to me about whatever it was you were going through?"

"I tried. You know. Sending subliminals. But I guess you didn't pick up."

I did not. In class, he was joyful. I had not taken the time to imagine what he was feeling outside of class. But the more he spoke on it, the more I could see what I had missed. Before his arrest, there had been a fire in his apartment building. What little he had was damaged when the firefighters came through the walls to get to the room next door. He got supplemental housing money that lasted about a week. After the fire, the bar where he worked as a cook closed down, and everyone lost their jobs. Without a job to pay for an apartment in the city, he was living with his mother out in the county, hitching rides to campus for class.

It took me a minute to gather my thoughts. The visiting room was swollen with sound. Shrill storytelling. Children pleading. Raucous laughing. It was like a sprawling family reunion stitched across too many families. I could not compete with the volume other than to match it. I didn't want to match it, but as I thought about the man getting put away for marijuana again, it was easier to get angry at the police than it was to get angry at myself for missing the story.

"This is bullshit! That cop had no right to search your motel room without a warrant!" The room went quiet. People near us began watching me with a mixture of alarm and curiosity.

"Easy," Terence whispered, placing a hand on my shoulder. I can't remember how the visit ended, but somehow it did, and I drove Terence home.

The next day, I bought one of those "sorry, you've hit a rough patch, but we're rooting for you" cards and put it in my folder for class. I was dreading telling everyone the news. How was I supposed to tell the diverted participants in particular that the one coaching them on how to stay out of jail was back in jail? At the end of class, I took out the card, held it up, and then began passing it around. When I told them Dean was in jail, they gasped. When I told them why—that he got busted for weed in Henrico—they groaned. Whatever embarrassment I felt going into that class dissipated in that collective groan.

In a letter, Dean thanked me for visiting. But he was also concerned. The court-appointed attorney was telling him he was facing ten years. It didn't seem right. He visited the law library and realized that his attorney was using the sentencing guidelines for cocaine! He'd also gotten the weight of the drug wrong. Dean asked if I could reach out to the Henrico Commonwealth's Attorney's Office to explain this to the prosecutor, and while I was at it, to tell them about the book, the program, and his service in the community.

I applied Mike's litmus test about public safety. I strained to see any reason for incarcerating Dean. I had never noticed any serious harm to himself or others coming from his using or selling weed. I contacted the attorney assigned to Dean's case. He complimented me for teaching people in jail, asked to see the book, and promised to take it into account during the trial. I closed my laptop and entertained the possibility that he might actually do it.

The courtroom was empty. Blond wood, dusty blue carpeting, a sour smell that I could not place. It was like a forlorn diner after hours. Nothing was cooking. No one was there. Just the officers, the flags, Dean's mother, and me. Dean came through a side door, handcuffed behind his back. With his eyes, he apologized. The deputy took out a tiny tool to loosen the chain. Dean's shoulders eased. Now he could breathe. He could handle paper and lean on the counsel's table.

His attorney had rough skin and restless eyes. His shirt struggled to stay tucked in over his paunch. With so few people in the courtroom, I could hear a little of what he was saying. He seemed amped on his own pep talk, telling Dean that this deal he had struck with the prosecution was a great deal, the best deal Dean would get, the best solution for the court. The prosecutor that I had emailed with was younger, taller, with a smooth, bald head and an olive complexion. He wore a shiny, collared shirt that was blindingly white and wrinkle-free. It was the kind of shirt that said, *I work out. You can't see it, but trust me, I work out.*

The defense attorney called me to the witness box. His questions were about Dean's character. Short passes from the quarterback. Quick and decisive. My job was to receive and run my story into the endzone of a light judgment—a drug program, time-served in jail, something like that. The prosecutor played a different game. He pulled some dates from the book about Dean's criminal history. He added these to the dates of crimes that were not in the book. Then he read the list chronologically.

"Dr. Coogan, are you aware of all of these charges?"

"Most of them."

"Do these charges not reveal the character of a persistent drug dealer? Mr. Turner has not changed, no matter his good intentions, his writing, or his good works in the community. He is nothing if not consistent. He has always been a drug dealer. He has always been a harmful presence in the community. Do you deny this?" I took a deep breath and let it out, searching for the right analytical register. I needed to speak in a way that the court could comprehend. It wasn't me speaking, but the office of a character witness.

"I think if you look again at that list, you'll see that the charges decrease in severity over time. They are not the same charges, the same drugs, or the same amounts. He did not receive the same sentences."

"But there is a pattern."

I wanted to turn the moral high ground back at him. Surely, you don't think selling marijuana is as dangerous to the community as violent crime? Surely, you don't think his older charges, some of which included firearms, fit into the same pattern as his more recent ones for using and selling marijuana? Or do you still subscribe to the now-discredited research characterizing marijuana as a gateway drug, hence a harm to the community?[45] Maybe you imagine Virginia's noncompliance with the other states that have legalized marijuana to be somehow morally just, not backward? I wanted to get into it. But what I wanted would not have been heard in the bureaucratic setting of the courtroom.

"The pattern I see is a man trying to do his best to change his life. He may be going slow, but he is going in the right direction. He is not harming anyone in the community now. Through his writing and service, he is actually helping the community."

Dean's mother was welling up watching me. I had just given all I could give. When I finished, the judge bid me to step down. Aside from the soft buzz of the overhead lights, it was dead quiet as I left the witness box. As I walked toward the gallery, I turned to look at the judge. He met my eyes briefly, then looked away. Maybe at some level, I had persuaded him that this was not a case worth prosecuting? He seemed embarrassed to be presiding over this drama. But what could he do? He did not make the law. When I sat down near Dean's mother, the prosecutor turned around and mouthed out *I'm sorry* for the cross-examination. That surprised me, too. Maybe it wasn't really him speaking, either. It was just his office denying mercy.

28
The Kids

Kelvin

Some of the best things that have happened to me in my adult life have come from *Writing Our Way Out*. Forming a brotherhood with the guys in the book. Speaking events. Even some jobs.

Before the book, I was just getting into trouble. Being able to go into a college classroom now and encourage people to spend some of their time helping kids means a lot to me. I like getting to speak to people who are curious enough and care enough to make a difference, so the next kid doesn't end up being like me. I like helping with the diversion program to keep people out of the system.

Being contacted to do a TED Talk put me off-kilter. I didn't feel too comfortable about it at all. So, when they contacted me to tell my story about going to jail, writing my story, getting out, and turning my life around, I reached out to Dave. And if he hadn't agreed to go out there with me, I never would have agreed to do it. I'd been onstage before, but not as an adult. I was onstage when I was a kid in elementary school, playing the dog catcher in *Annie*. That was my biggest role so far. And I danced in the talent show at Henderson Middle School. I knew what it felt like being up there under that spotlight. But that's different. You don't have to be speaking, looking at people, or engaging the crowd.

Once I got into it and got over the nerves, I was fine. And little did I know, but that night, my next employer was in the audience: Mike Maruca, the principal at Anna Julia Cooper School. He'd brought some of the eighth graders to Collegiate High School, where they were hosting the TED Talks. They saw us up there, and my story must have touched the kids, most of them impoverished from rough parts of town. Mike reached out to Dave to get us out to the school to present, and we ended up starting a writing workshop with the kids.

I did not go into that situation thinking that Black kids from the projects weren't as smart as other kids. But to find out, they actually seemed smarter! They were definitely smarter than me or any kids I grew up with. They wrote like adults who should already be published. They shared like I know I couldn't do at that age. The way the school treated them while we were there made me feel like it wasn't even real, like they were just putting on a show for us. But the more times we went, the more I came to see that the school really was doing what the kids needed. The classes were small. The teachers really cared. And it was a private school, so, you know, they could do things the way they wanted.

I'm never going to forget the little girl who said I reminded her of her uncle. I've still got her paper somewhere in my house—a poem she wrote for our workshop that made me cry. When she read it out loud in class, she cried, too, because she didn't see her uncle anymore. That was one of my favorite moments, knowing I helped another kid.

Then there was the boy who always sat by the window, who read a poem that was supposed to be about your hero. He wrote, "When I think of my hero, I just think of the opposite of my dad." And he listed all the things. He was angry when he read it, but I remember later telling him that people tell me I'm a good dad because of the things I learned *not* to do from my dad. I'm a better father because he showed me what not to do. I told him it could work out that way for him, too.

When I was much younger, still in school, I went looking for my daddy. I ain't had no father in my life, but I knew who he was. I wound up calling his house. And the person who answered was Kim, my little sister. She told me who she was and what was going on in the home. I can't remember exactly how she said it, but she told me as a young girl how it was. She let me know that things with my daddy weren't how they seemed. That's how I met my sister. She told me not to look for what you're looking for from our daddy—he wasn't going to be that father to me. From day one, she's always been looking out for her big brother. I've always looked up to my little sister after that. She had the courage to tell me the truth.

She's always had my back. One time, when I got out of prison, I stayed in Kim's spare room. When I was volunteering at Black Top Kings and Queens, coaching basketball, she cooked for all the kids. But it's crazy. When she's going through something, she won't tell me. She'll tell Dennis, my brother from another mother. He's like family to us. They call each other brother and sister. I still admire my little big sister. She's been through some of the same things as me in the streets. But it hurts sometimes that I can't be there for her.

When our writing program at the school had run its course, Mike, the principal, came to me and told me they were adding a new building and would need a maintenance guy. He wanted me to interview. I left Main Street Realty when I got that job at Anna Julia Cooper School.

When I was young, I always imagined working at a school. I knew I wouldn't be a teacher. Maybe I'd be a counselor, or that guy walking around pushing a trash can, joking with the kids. That was what drew me to the job. It was something I had envisioned for myself.

I was a presence for the kids, and they liked me. But after a few years, Mike Maruca told me it wasn't working, the way I did maintenance and the way they wanted to run the school. I still don't quite know why they let me go. The answers they gave weren't clear. But it hurt me for a while.

I still coach basketball for the school that fired me. I do it for the kids. Like Bones. That's my future Hall-of-Famer. My power forward center/team leader. Kids at the school call her Bones, I think, because she wears a lot of black and white, like a Goth-type kid. It's a cool basketball name. But she's been through a lot living in Mosby Court public housing. The apartment near hers got shot up, and all the kids had to run out the back. So now she and her family are going to move out of there. Recently, she texted me at seven in the morning: "Have a great day, Mr. KB!" I wrote back right away. "Great days are for great people. You enjoy your day. I am still Bones' number one fan."

Given the opportunity, I would do a lot more coaching. I like those connections. One of my favorite moments coaching at AJC was when I was running late for a game. When I got there, we were losing terribly. Hadn't scored. And the head coach was looking furious. Red in the face. When she saw me come in, she just looked at me and said, "KB, you got 'em. I'm gone!" And she walked to the other part of the bench.

We didn't win. It was too late to turn the corner. But I really felt the love that day. Those kids went all out for me. Scored a few baskets. Felt good about themselves. Even though we got blown out, that week was our turnaround.

We started playing better as a team, and they really started looking forward to the next season.

My own kids are a different story. My oldest son, Lil Kelvin, didn't start off living with me, so he had a different view from the others. He was always coming into the city from the counties to see me. He understands me better now because he's older, and he comes around on Sundays to play ball, which is a good thing. But I don't think he really sees me. He has kids of his own, and I spend more time being happy that he has a good connection with his kids than I spend worrying whether he has one with me.

My other son, Rell, basically dresses and acts like me. He wears bucket hats like me. He's been locked up like me. He's more of a basketball player like me. But Lil Kelvin's the one who comes to play with me. I ain't tripping. I know where it comes from. The older you get, the less relevant you are to young people. They won't see it until they get older. They have to be allowed to live their lives. I always want my kids to make their own decisions. I'm proud of both of my sons. They're good fathers. Good family men.

My mentality about parenting is ever-changing. There are just so many more mentalities to the person I am now. I've written my way out of a lot of things, not just the street mentality. I used to be someone who didn't believe in mental health. Now, after all the talking and sharing that we've been through with this book, I feel like I need some counseling. So, you know, I've changed a lot.

I also see now that I can handle more than I can't handle. I've been able to be broke and have bills due and not go out and do the wrong thing. I know God puts more on the people he knows can handle it, and if I buck, that means I'm not doing what I'm supposed to be doing. I need to show I can manage what's been given to me so I can get my reward at the next level. That's what I'm battling to do now—to hold on to the strength I need, knowing there's going to be more for me on the other side.

29
The Perfect Fit

Dave

Spring, 2019. Alligator shoes perched on pedestals. Suit jackets lined the racks. The fedoras were stacked, ready for heads. A pair of pants and a tape measure lay on the counter. It was Saturday morning at Stockpile. The shop was not open yet, but Stan's interview for a sales position was about to begin. I had not planned on staying. I just came to make the introduction. But when Pastor Harris gestured for me to sit in the elegant armchair, I sat.

Harris has a way of leaning in when he is about to render judgment. His shoulders slope. His forehead flexes. His eyes grow wide with critical awareness. I knew this look from the conversations we'd had about G, who had done the ministry with Harris, selling shirts and ties door-to-door; he did not think G was really trying to stay out of the streets. I knew it from the meeting we'd had at my church with Terence, where Harris told us the story about buying a guy's crack to prevent him from using it and then flushing it down the toilet. And I knew it from a meeting I'd had with him and Dean, and the rest of the people he had assembled in Harvey's Progressive Barber Shop for his mentorship program. He'd leaned in when I gave a definition of mentoring that was much different from everyone else's. Theirs were about flexing their authority and holding guys accountable. Mine was about listening and asking questions.

When Stan's job interview began, Harris revealed to him that he had run a criminal background check on him. He knew about his last incarceration and the damage he did to his girlfriend's car. He wanted to know if he had any regrets. Stan, who had been reclining in his armchair, sat up and planted his forearms on his legs.

"Yes, my actions put me in harm's way." But he would not disavow his actions. The car was his. It was just registered in his girlfriend's name. When she told him she would not let him use it anymore, he felt trapped. He had to defend himself.

Harris leaned in as far as he could go. Sunlight spilled through the shop's front window. A mirror caught it and tossed it over to the dress shirts.

"But that was in the past," I suggested. "You don't have that kind of stress in your life now."

"Yeah, no doubt," Stan confirmed. "I am in a much better place now."

Harris continued to stare. Stan looked across the room.

"Man, I like this place," he said, nodding as he spoke. "There's a spirit here. This place has a purpose."

"What's that?" Harris asked.

"To welcome the people, to show them the possibilities."

Harris leaned back and relaxed his face. They had figured out their roles in the conversation, or what the sociologist Erving Goffman calls "the definition of a situation." Goffman explains that "when an individual projects a definition of the situation," he "exerts a moral demand on others." He obliges them "to value and treat him" in a way that people like him "have a right to expect."[46] Once established, this definition guides future interactions. What Stan was saying was that he was not just an ex-offender asking to wait on customers; he was there to welcome people. It was not about salesmanship but about fellowship. He got the job.

After Stan got the job, I began stopping by Stockpile on my way home from campus. It was right on Main Street in Shockoe Bottom. I liked visiting the store. It was like a social club open to the public. A bar without the drinks. A barbershop without the clippers. A sociable place with men lingering long after they had made their purchases. Stan was right. There was a spirit to the place.

I stood off to the side one time. Stan was alone with a customer. He was young and heavyset and gearing up to marry. He had already picked out the suit. Now he had to pick the tie, belt, and shoes. Stan waved me over. I congratulated the groom. He thanked me and smiled, but was either too shy to say anything else or lost in thought about the wedding. Stan turned around to gather some belts. When they were neatly arranged on the counter, he peered over his reading glasses, inviting the groom to choose.

"You remind me of my father-in-law," the groom said quietly, as much to himself as to us. "You're old-school." It seemed to comfort him, the comparison. Stan was old enough to be the man's father. And compared to the groom, who was dressed casually in jeans and a T-shirt, Stan, in his olive slacks and braided brown belt, looked old-school. "Which one do you think I should get?"

"This one," Stan said, touching the belt in the middle. "It's on point with the color of your suit, and we can match it easily with whatever shoes you want." The groom nodded and turned toward the shoes.

"Hold up. Try it on," Stan directed. Slowly, the young man threaded the belt around his ample waist. Stan stepped back and touched his chin, appraising, as the man fastened the buckle.

"You want me to add another hole? Just in case?" A familiar caution came over the groom's face. It seemed like this was the kind of decision he had made before, but had not thought about until now. He nodded, a little pained and relieved all at once.

"Yeah, we'd better," he said as he freed the belt from his body. Stan reached for the hole puncher. Then the man and I watched as Stan positioned the belt in the machine, raised the handle, and broke through the leather with a satisfying thwack, like dough thrown down on the counter.

The next week, when I visited, Stan was standing near the register pressing a toothpick between his lips. He was listening to Pastor Harris talking about his ministry at the jail.

"What more could we do to help guys getting out?" Harris asked. "What do guys really need?"

"A job," Stan answered.

"But how could they interview without the right clothes?" Harris continued. Stan took the toothpick out of his mouth. Harris pointed toward one of the suits on a mannequin.

"What if we fit them for a suit in jail so that they could pick one up when they were released?"

"And what if Dave was there to help them write a resume? Something to put into that suit pocket," Stan added. I liked where this was going. It was not something I'd thought much about given the comfortable clothes I wear, but maybe clothes do make the man?

In a study about reentry, Liam Martin observed that people who have "deeply ingrained prison habits and dispositions" often struggle when they have to "confront new patterns of daily life in the outside world." They stare hard at people they don't know. They withdraw from casual kindnesses, avoid eye contact, and resist authority. To compensate, some start "tailoring their dress and speech to strategically perform a version of the reformed self that corresponds with employer expectations."[47] Change can come from within. But sometimes, an external change in behavior can give the mind time to catch up to the body.

Stan began rehearsing a speech he would give to the men in jail who would take this program that we were brainstorming. He knew what guys in there cared about and worried about but would not talk about. He grew animated as he warmed to his themes of preparation, presentation, and power. I considered the salesman speaking. He wore a black pork pie hat, a black velvet suit jacket, and a white button-down shirt dotted in black. An ivory handkerchief was rolled loosely like a scroll and nestled in the breast pocket. Above it was a red carnation. When he gestured with both arms, I saw the pearl cuff links. Was this the reformed self or the performance of one?

I was at the dentist's office, waiting for my son's appointment to finish, when Stan called in a bad mood. I stepped outside and began walking as I listened. He had asked Harris for an advance on his salary to pay off his court fines. Harris agreed to pay the fine, but not as an advance. He would pay it himself and deduct the principal from Stan's next paycheck. Reluctantly, Stan agreed. The problem came later when he got to the court clerk's office to give them the check. There was a late fee. He needed another fifty dollars. He called Harris, asking him to send the rest of the money through Western Union. Harris sent it. But the next day, he made Stan do a drug test. They closed the shop, drove to a facility, filled out some paperwork, and the nurse sent Stan into the bathroom to pee in a cup. He returned moments later with an empty cup.

"You knew what they would find, then," I said.

"I know my rights, Dave." He would not say if he was using drugs. He would not say if he'd used any of that money from court to buy drugs. He sounded proud, unwilling to give any ground. He also sounded as if he had been busted using, but could not admit it to himself. He thought he could manage the lie through the cover of the role he had constructed for himself as a salesman and soldier in the ministry of welcoming people to Stockpile to show them the possibilities in life. Goffman might say that he had been "taken in by his own act," and convinced that the "impression of reality" he had created was "the one and only reality."[48] But there were flaws in the performance that had called his agency into question, flaws that Harris caught: the sudden, urgent need for money and then the empty cup.

Harris called me the next day to tell me his version of the same story. I agreed with him that Stan was probably using again, and that was not good for Stan or for business. But I reminded him that he was trying to run a ministry for ex-offenders as well as a business. This was why he had taken on the challenge of hiring Stan. This was a part of the experience. He agreed to give Stan another chance. Weeks later, he called to tell me he regretted it. He had discovered some items missing from the shop: embroidered T-shirts, sunglasses, dress shirts, slacks, even alligator shoes, the good ones with the jewels embedded on the tongue. He had footage from the security cameras of Stan "taking out the trash" to the alley and returning in the evening with a woman who drove him there to pick it up. I called Stan to confront him.

"That man's disorganized. He just lost track of that merchandise. He probably sold it and forgot to record it sold."

"He has footage."

"Of me taking out the trash?"

"He tells me he saw someone wearing one of those embroidered T-shirts downtown and asked him where he got it." It got quiet on the other end of the line. "The guy said he got it on the street. Mr. Harris asked who sold it to him. The guy described you, Stan."

"It's not like that. We had a system. I was supposed to be out modelling the clothes. The walking mannequin, we called it. I did sell a shirt to a guy that way. He saw me wearing one, asked about it, and I sold him one."

"You never gave Harris the money."

"It's just one shirt."

"I don't care if it was ten shirts. It's wrong."

Harris called again to ask for my help retrieving the merchandise. A mutual friend of his and Stan's—Pastor Whitehead—was called in for backup. Whitehead arranged with Stan a day and time when he was home so we could retrieve the merchandise. The three of us drove in our own cars. I parked in front of the apartment building. Harris and Whitehead were parked a block away. It felt like a stakeout. I called Stan. He came out into the street with a large duffel bag and brought it over to my car. I got out and popped the trunk. He dropped it in. We didn't talk much. Stan asked me to bring back the duffel, then reconsidered and disappeared back into his apartment.

I pulled away from the curb and into the empty street, heading back to Stockpile. Harris and Whitehead eased out to follow me. I got a call. It was Harris. He asked me to stop on the next block. He would get the stuff there instead of back at the shop. I stopped, opened the trunk, and stood back as he went through the bag, creating a small storm of shirts and slacks until he extracted the jeweled alligator shoes. He let out a heavy sigh, zipped up the duffel, and leaned toward me.

"You need to be careful who you recommend," he said.

Was Stan not keyed in to fashion? Good looking and persuasive? Good with people? "Sometimes," Goffman observes, "when we ask whether a fostered impression is true or false, we really mean to ask whether or not the performer is authorized to give the performance in question."[49] I believe, in the beginning, Stan was so authorized. But when he started stealing and using, and lying, he lost that authorization. Still, when he helped that groom into his wedding suit and punched that extra hole in his belt, I know what I saw—not just between a customer and his new clothes, but between Stan and a shy young man he took care of that day. The perfect fit.

30

Black Lives Matter

Dave

Spring/Summer, 2020. It thundered the day the crane pried Stonewall Jackson from his pedestal near First Baptist Church. This was not the white man in uniform who killed George Floyd. But public protests over that excruciating, nine-minute murder of an unarmed Black man in Minneapolis made it painfully clear to people in Richmond that monuments to the Lost Cause could no longer be dismissed as some archaic petulance—these were living legacies to white supremacy.

Stan had called the day after the protests began. He was impressed that so many white people were involved.

"They're peeling off layers they didn't know they had, Dave. White people shedding!" In my mind's eye, I could see his brow flexing into the thought, head tilting left and then centering again as his eyes steadied before the vision. I was walking through the city as we talked.

"Not all white people," he added. At Richfield Place Apartments, where he had worked as a maintenance man, he told me that he had to challenge his supervisor, a white man in his sixties who was just as racist as could be. Stan told him that the protests happening up and down the country and in Richmond, up and down Monument Avenue, were about people who think like him.

"Should I have told him that? Yes. Should I have told him that? No. That's the dichotomy. I'm going to suffer if I tell the truth. And if I don't tell the truth, I'm still going to suffer, because it's just going to burn me up inside. I believe in confrontation."

I walked through a different dichotomy as he talked. A Black man in a janitor's uniform was scrubbing the spray-painted "Black Lives Matter" off the side of the courthouse. I could only see his back. I could only intuit his perspective. Was it self-erasure or just a job? Across the street, smashed glass littered the sidewalk beneath a glass window with "All Cops . . . Bastards" spray-painted on it. Someone had thrown a brick at the verb. Spidery lines strung out from the hole, either negating the claim or reinforcing it.

"The cops are making these protests worse," Stan continued. "They're not listening! They're coming out with pepper spray and batons when they should have water bottles and pamphlets of information to get us toward a solution!"

"I totally agree."

"Okay, check this out. I've got the topic for your next book. You ready?" He paused dramatically.

"Hit me."

"From white to human."

"Oh, wow."

"You understand what I'm saying? You know what I mean?" It was the kind of topic that broke itself down.

"This is all new to them. They need a guide. And you're the perfect one for the job. You've been putting yourself in that position for years now! How long has it been?"

"Since I've known you—since we started the project? Fifteen years."

"Damn! They got to listen to you."

I was not so sure. On my walk home from campus the night before, I met a crowd in Monroe Park. The mood was festive as people greeted each other and geared up with their BLM signs. I am temperamentally mismatched for protest. The shouting, the emotional intensity, the monotony of slogans, the imminent violence—it alarms me. But that night, I challenged myself to get out of my comfort zone. I mumbled along with the chants. Most people around me stuck to the script. But others began ranging over the procession with a wilder kind of desire, a harder cadence, and spirited expletives. A giddy abandon gripped the crowd as they began blocking traffic on Belvidere, the busy street bisecting campus. I watched from the curb with a pounding heart as they did their thing. Then I took a different path home.

"They got to listen to you!" Stan said again. "You know why?" He paused to set me up.

"Why?"

"You took the time to hear our stories. That's the humanity right there."

"Thanks, Stan."

"All right, I'm gone, Dave."

I kept walking. I stopped under the awning of a diner at 3rd and Main, across the street from where the nonprofit Offender Aid and Restoration used to be located. This is the nonprofit that got me started teaching writing at the jail all those years ago. The building is a tattoo parlor now. While I reminisced and reflected on the protests, I heard an older Black man in an oversized red T-shirt yelling at a younger Black man with a small backpack. There was no one else around. The younger man walked off suddenly. The older man went after him, yelling.

"You try to rob me? Man, I'll fuck you up! Get your ass back here." He followed him into the big vacant parking lot across the street. Then, out of nowhere, a police car crossed the lot diagonally, slowly, and stopped to intercept them.

"Good!" the older one shouted. "Good! Now they can arrest your ass!"

The cop parked and got out of the car. He was young and white and stood before them, relaxed, unmoved, maybe even bored. He just presented himself and listened as the two men told their sides of the story. I was going to walk off. But with the news of George Floyd's death in my head, I put my finger over the camera icon on my phone and put myself on notice.

"What do you think happened?" I asked Stan when I called later that afternoon to tell him the story. I paused to set him up.

"What?"

"Nothing!"

"Yeah," he said with a shrug, like he had heard this story before, like he had even been in it before, where the flame of a conflict does not match its heat.

"The cop just let the old guy wear himself out. Then he got back in his car and drove away."

"What happened to the young guy?"

"He just stood there. Then the old guy lunged back across the street and kicked the young guy's little laundry basket."

"What?"

"You know, the kind of thing they give out at the shelter. Little basket with toothpaste, deodorant, that kind of thing. The young guy waited for the old guy to finish kicking it and cursing him, then he went over there to pick it all up."

"So that's what they were beefing about? Some bullshit?"

"Yeah. But it made me think of what you said earlier. The police should be opening up dialogue instead of shutting it down." As soon as I gave the moral, though, I wanted to take it back. "I suppose this wasn't a real dialogue. The old guy was just yelling. The cop didn't really do much."

"Yeah, but he listened. He took the time."

31
Quitting

Naji

When I realized it was over with Cassandra, I knew I needed to get help, so I checked into a rehab facility in Arlington, Virginia. With nothing but the best intentions and the right frame of mind, I committed to completing the program. Little did I know, the absolute worst thing that could ever happen to someone in my situation was coming for me. It utterly annihilated my newfound resolve.

In 2021, COVID-19 was running rampant all over the country. When I arrived at the Phoenix House in Arlington, it was packed to capacity with mostly young guys escaping the streets, the law, their parents, or all of the above. I felt odd being around so many people more than half my age, but I quickly settled in and focused on recovery.

After a few days, I became familiar with the facility. I spent my time in their computer room, where I could sit and take care of business, like ordering a new ID or reapplying for my Social Security and birth certificate cards, things I had lost. One morning, I was sitting at the terminal when a young man walked up and asked me if I had received my stimulus. I had no clue what he was talking about.

"What stimulus?" I replied.

"Oh, you don't know!" he said, eyes wide, amazed. He went on to explain to me the craziest thing I had ever heard in my life. According to him, the government was giving out $1,400 to every American citizen because of the COVID crisis. I looked at him as if he had lost his mind.

"Stop playing," I said. He scanned the room and called on another guy.

"Yo, Mike, didn't I just get you $1,400?"

Mike looked up and said, "Yeah. So?" Other guys in the room were looking over, too, and nodding.

At that point, I went from being suspicious to curious. "How long does it take?"

To my surprise, he said Scoot over, let me do this for you. I jumped up and gave him the terminal. In about ten minutes, he looked back up at me. "You're good. You should receive something in the mail in the next seven to ten days."

I got a FedEx package approximately a week later. I opened it, and inside was what appeared to be a debit card. This can't be true! There can't be any money on it, I thought. But when I called the number on the card to check the balance, I was informed that I had $1,400. I almost dropped the phone.

Much as I tried to combat it, my addictive brain automatically planned an excuse to leave and get high. I understood exactly what was happening, but I had no fortitude to stop it. How could I convince myself that I was going to stay and complete the program now? The money was burning a hole in my pocket. All I could think about was getting high.

It was approximately 12:00 p.m. when I received the card. I held out until two the next morning. I packed everything I had and told the on-duty technician downstairs that I had a family problem and had to leave. I caught a Greyhound bus back to Hampton, where I immediately sought out any drug I could find to get high. The money lasted about a month. Before I knew it, I was on the street—broke, homeless, and completely disgusted with myself.

Being homeless does something to your spirit. For me, it robbed me of my ability to correct myself. This pattern of behavior continued for a couple of years. I would end up in either hospitals or rehabs, only to return to the drug-criminal lifestyle that got me there in the first place. I was completely lost, with no hope in sight. In spite of the difficulties I was experiencing, I felt as though I was a very strong person, but if I am to be honest, suicide crossed my mind on more than one occasion.

Emporia, Virginia, was another stop at a crisis intervention home. I'm not entirely sure how I got there. When I completed their program, I found employment at Boar's Head meat manufacturers. The pay was good, but the work was extremely difficult. After a couple of months, I developed carpal tunnel in both hands and was laid off. I moved back to the Tidewater region and ended up in a crisis stabilization program in Portsmouth, in what was supposed to be a sober living house, but turned out to be a crack house. From there, I moved on to Chesapeake, where I experienced the same thing.

Over and over again, I would find myself in a rehab or hospital. I was only on the streets for a couple of months. Slowly, street drugs began to lose their appeal for me. The allure was fading. The people I had to deal with on a daily basis were savage. The daily hustle to find money to support my habit was taxing. The constant moving, losing my personal belongings—the high started to feel not worth the time and effort. Somehow, I found myself just south of Richmond in Petersburg in another program. I was still using, but for the first time in my life, I knew I was on the verge of quitting.

After a few months, I found myself involved with a woman who happened to be strung out on fentanyl. It was also the first time that narcissism entered my vocabulary. She was a little younger than me, and I felt as though, maybe through helping her, I could help myself. I didn't consider that the blind cannot lead the blind. I was alone. She was alone. And it became a comfort for us to be together. Her addiction was much greater than my own. There were many occasions when I had to facilitate bringing her back to life. I couldn't convince her to leave it all alone. After all, I was strung out on crack cocaine. How could I ever convince anybody to stop using when I was using myself?

Fentanyl is a beast. People were dropping like fried flies all around me, yet it was becoming more popular by the minute. She and I would sit up at night talking about what we needed to do in order to quit. One day, she sincerely asked me if I would help her quit. I told her I would, and that I would quit using my drug of choice, also. I decided we would move out of the city, where temptation to use was everywhere. We moved to Chesterfield County, got a hotel room, and stayed inside for a few days so that she could kick her habit. There were no physiological cravings coming off of cocaine; it was mostly mental, so I was good. But she was seriously struggling.

One morning, she started a big argument. I immediately knew this was her attempt to break away from me so that she could find some fentanyl. To get what she wanted, she knew she had to get me out of the way. And for this, she went to the extreme. She called the Chesterfield Police and told them I was abusing her. She told them I had a gun and was threatening to kill her.

The police arrived and, seeing me with a Caucasian woman, didn't hesitate to put handcuffs on me and put me in the back of the truck. They took me to see a judge, where I was charged with domestic assault, although there was no evidence—no gun or witnesses that heard anything—to suggest that something violent was happening in the room. It seemed my only crime was dating a white woman.

My court date was set for thirty days out. I knew she wouldn't come to court; she'd gotten me out of the way, and that was all she wanted. The thirty days' jail time flew by, with no contact with anybody who knew her or me. When I got out, the first place I went to look for her was a hotel in Petersburg where we'd both stayed at one point. The first person to recognize me came up and asked me if I'd heard? I said no, what happened? She said, "Your girl is dead. She overdosed."

The way she said it, so matter-of-fact, sickened me. She'd known this girl well; they'd gotten high together. Yet in her face there was no emotion, no sympathy. I couldn't believe it! I was stunned! My mind couldn't fathom not seeing this girl again. I wasn't in love with her, but I cared about her deeply. How could you interact with someone on a daily basis and not feel some sense of loss?

The realization hit me like a ton of bricks: These people I'd been associating with weren't human—at least they didn't behave like normal human beings. Was this what it meant to be an addict? It was the ugliest thing I've ever seen in my life. At that moment, I decided I had to get far away from this shit.

My friend's death shook me. That was the catalyst for the change that would take place in my life. I'd told her on many occasions that death was stalking her. I could see it clearly. But she couldn't. She was battling demons and had no way out, and nobody to turn to. With me incarcerated, the wolves were able to close in on her, and she didn't have a chance.

I was mad at the drug dealers. I was mad at the drugs. And I was mad at myself for even being associated with any of it. I was mad that we both were born and raised in a cesspool that resents human development and is dead-set against real progress of the mind and moral character—a place where evil vices exist legally for citizens to resort to when beaten down by the drudgery of existing as debt slaves. Our lives are reduced to being mere cogs in a corporate machine, the only escape being drugs and death!

The values of this country are tainted and corrupt. Jiddu Krishnamurti said it best: "It is no measure of health to be well adjusted to a profoundly sick society." Even the people who appear to be flourishing in this insane asylum of abuse and social indoctrination are like a physically attractive woman whose brain is riddled with cancer. America appears beautiful, but it represents the sickest society ever to exist on the planet! I wasn't born an addict; I was made one. My friend died an addict because it was the natural end of the life of misery she was brought up in and subjected to. There is a lack of recognition in this country of the collective abuse and social indoctrination of its citizens.

Seeing this play out in the lives of everyone I knew put me in fight-or-flight mode. I refused to become a statistic like so many others. I decided I was going to fight till my last breath! I made the sincere decision to stop using drugs of any kind, even pharmaceuticals. I was diabetic, so insulin was a necessity, but as soon as I could figure out how to stop that, I would. Big pharma has become the new drug dealers, and I wasn't going to substitute street drugs for pharmaceutical ones. Purpose and connection would be the cure for my dysfunction, and following the tenets of my faith to the letter would be the roadmap to my success.

> Allah states: Qur'an, Al-'Asr, Surah 103: 1-3 By (the Token of) Time (through the ages), verily Man is in loss, except such as have Faith, and do righteous deeds, and (join together) in the mutual teaching of Truth, and of Patience and Constancy.

I know no other avenue of success. I have been clean for a year now, and my purpose is to spread the message of true recovery in everything I do. This is the purpose Allah has blessed me with, and I am grateful that I have been given the chance to die in a state of peaceful submission to his will. Islam!

32
Legacy

Dean

When I think about my life, I think about all the things I've been able to overcome in this short period of time. I've survived being shot three different times. One of the shootings was at point-blank range. I've been stabbed a few times. I survived four stints in the Virginia Department of Corrections. I've been homeless. I've been fortunate enough to witness a Black president. I've had my mental state tested on several occasions. I've also had to endure some of the most painful experiences: family and friends passing away.

As I'm writing this piece for our new book, looking back over my life, I can't help but think about my grandmother, Grace Royal, who was the backbone of the family. If only she could see what she has inspired and the legacy she left behind. Her kids are doing well, but it's her grandkids that are putting the stamp on shit. Most of her grands are living safe, healthy, and happy lives. Don't let me stop there. There's a bunch of success and hard work. I could go on and on about all the master's degrees and business degrees and business owners in the family, but I won't. Let's just say, we in the building!

I finally got to witness one of my kids come into the world and take their first breath, and it was really something special. It was a little extra special because I was finally getting a son. D'Anthony is now ten. The last piece to the puzzle. That's my little man. My little soldier. I want him to have a better life, a safer life, better opportunities than me to win. I'm going to make sure he doesn't have to go through what I've gone through. I definitely don't want my son to experience the prison system. I can't expect racism to vanish because not everyone is going to like you, see it your way, or agree with you, so I must prepare my son for what he's going to face. My job is to make sure he's ready for whatever comes his way.

I'm the perfect dad for the job. I'm double dangerous and super blessed. The reason I say this is that most of the obstacles he's going to face, I've already faced head-on. Gang member? Check. Drug dealer? Check. Been to the belly of the beast? Check. It's more, but you get the picture. I can go on forever, but I'm not here to glorify the awful things I did. It was wrong. It was dumb. I helped ruin my neighborhood. I helped ruin people's lives, and I regret it. So now I'm on the other side of the spectrum.

This is why I'm writing, so someone can read this and make a better decision with their life. You don't have to join that gang. You don't have to pull that trigger. You don't have to sell those drugs. Trust me. It's okay to work at McDonald's. It's okay to walk away from a fight or take that loss. Guess what? You live another day. You get to go home to your family. You get to live your life as a free man or woman. It took me some time to really understand that. You need to know this and hear from a real OG, a person who has been knocked down on a few occasions but manages to withstand the storm.

I know what it's like to wake up broke, hungry, and not knowing which way to turn. Trust me! That shit starts to fuck with your mentality, with your manhood, how you see yourself as a father, a husband, a protector, and a provider. You start to question yourself. You start to look within yourself. Why can't you get it right or get the breaks? I'm here to tell you that you can accomplish whatever is in your sights.

Listen, I had a stretch where I kept getting into trouble. I kept catching BS cases, and they kept me going back and forth in courtrooms and in and out of these judges' faces. Eventually, it started taking its toll on me, my family, and my relationship with my kids. My oldest daughter started to act out because I couldn't provide a stable environment, so she could be happy. If I'd had my shit together, I would have been in a position to offer that. There are things we don't see that kids see. Or we miss them because we are too caught up in our foolishness.

I wasted eleven and a half years of my life dealing with prisons, courts, judges, lawyers, and these streets, still coming up empty. I got a little something accomplished each time I came home, but the point of the matter is that I had to keep starting over. It never got any easier. You have to prove yourself to people. You have to gain people's trust again. You have to reestablish yourself.

When I look back on my life, there are a lot of things I would do differently. I can't change the past, but I can definitely have something to say about my future. I learned to be patient, realizing that I'm in full control of this ship. The only way I'm going to weather the storm is if I get rid of the dead weight and change course so I can have a clearer path to happiness and success. I might have to get rid of people who aren't contributing to my happiness or success. If that means family members gotta get cut off, so be it. If I have to get rid of the toxic girlfriend who doesn't see my vision, or friends who always seem to have a negative impact on my life, they must go!

The last time I got myself into trouble with the law over marijuana was the most degrading thing I've had to experience. Number one: I was back in the system and away from my family. Number two: Living in the worst possible conditions. Number three: I felt like a loser. I started to wonder if my life would only be this. It took a toll on my mental but once I realized that I would only be incarcerated for a short period of time, I began planning my comeback. I began planning my future, and I began to ask God for forgiveness, to give me the strength to erase my wrongs and pursue a stronger foundation for my family. So I focused all my attention on building up "me." I haven't looked back since.

I wrote down a plan, and I stuck to it. I read my plan to myself over and over until it was natural to me. The other thing I came to grips with was my expectations. I knew it wouldn't happen overnight, so I said to myself, I don't care how long it takes me. Just enjoy the ride. Enjoy the journey because there are going to be some bumps. Just know they won't last forever. Let's get it!

Once I learned how to be patient, take my time, still being relentless but understanding that it's a process I must go through, that's when things began to pick up. The light started to glow. My confidence became unbreakable, and regardless of how many noes I got from people, there were more yeses. I started this journey I'm on when I came home at the end of 2019. It's been a lot of heartbreak, but my grandmother didn't raise no punk, no quitter, so I pushed through all the shit and obstacles in my way. Plus, I had the almighty and most high right by my side. There was nothing I couldn't crush: living in a halfway house, living in a rooming house with bedbugs biting me, a rooming house where people were overdosing.

This journey would have broken the average man. But my guardian angel would whisper to me, "Never give up." So I kept pushing. Trust me! A few times, I thought about ending it. The depression is real. I couldn't go out like that, though. Now I'm on my bully shit. Striving to accomplish my goals. And nothing or no one is getting in my way. See you at the top.

33

Road to Damascus

Stan

It is Saturday. I am six hundred miles away from the place I have called home my entire existence. I am in the Wayside Christian Mission in Louisville, Kentucky, because in Richmond, Virginia, with a stem in my mouth and a Bic lighter in hand, I was repeatedly lighting the fuse of my demise. With each flicker and each deep pull, my vision of who I am became distorted. So now I am a runaway slave of addiction.

My transplantation back into the wilderness of society in October 2015 didn't go so well. And that's how I came to be sitting with pen and paper and my thoughts in a greenhouse of recovery. I needed to put myself back into a shallow pot of confinement. Not prison but something close to it. A recovery home. Wayside. Here, I wait patiently for my appointment with purpose, with all things the Great I AM. Over the last few years, I've drifted away from that purpose, and the heartbeat of joy has grown fainter and fainter. Recovery in this story means rediscovering on a more profound level who I am in conjunction with the Great I AM. God, grant me the insight to share what is within me. Let's take this journey together.

Before I boarded the Greyhound in Richmond, I was employed by a paving company in Rockville, Virginia. We were a crew of maybe eight men that paved state roads all night long. Our crew's foreman was named Neville, and he had thirty-plus years of paving under his belt. This man's only goal each night was to take us to the finish line safely and efficiently.

Neville was more than a boss to me. When I was hungry, his family fed me. I shared what I was dealing with, and he took the time to listen. Ville was an African American man with a dark hue. A strong chiseled character. A working man. But his best asset was he was a family man.

The next two crew members were also instrumental in my journey on the road to Damascus. They, too, helped me get to this place of true purpose in the promised land of sobriety. In their wisdom, Elijah and Keith were like stilts; they lifted me out of myself so that I could see myself. Keith fucked me up one night when he said, "You're disappearing." That was how much weight I was losing because of my addiction. I felt love and abasement all in one blink. But day by day Keith fed me words of encouragement and bologna sandwiches. Soul food.

Eli was younger than Keith and more energetic. He had a life I desire even today: children that he gladly takes care of, a woman that gladly cares for him. Man, you should have seen some of his lunches! Shrimp. Steaks. You name it, she fed this young brother with respect and love, and he shared that soul food with me. Damn, it was seasoned with the power of care and concern. Each meal was a letter from God.

The last person on the crew I will write about was Craig, the prize-winning bull. Much stronger than the other crew members, he was capable of leading the crew in any task. A true gallant and gladiator twined together. We clashed often about me. He had ways of reminding me he knew that I was getting high. And he was a bully about it.

When an addict keeps it to himself, he's still sharing it in how he looks, he's sharing it in how he smells, he's sharing it in what he wears. You don't need to ask a person if he's getting high. You can see that shit. You can see rhythms and patterns and routines being broken. Craig was a bull coming after me for those reasons, but every time he charged at me, I moved that muleta away just like a matador.

Addiction is stagnation. Stagnant water becomes poisonous water. If I get stagnant, there's going to be some bacteria on me. Some poison. Some toxicities involved. And I'll get high. Stagnation always leads to relapse.

Yes, my weight was disappearing, but inside, in my heart, I was always strong enough to stand my ground. Those clashes with Craig gave me a major lesson about loving my brother despite his actions and words toward me. I concluded that love never fails. Thank you, Craig, Elijah, Keith, and Neville for strengthening me on my journey to discover my life of true purpose.

* * *

What I liked about being in recovery at Wayside in Kentucky was seeing the different approaches counselors took. I enjoyed NA meetings once I understood their language. At first, I didn't know what step one was, step two, step three, any of that. But once I could decode their language, I understood that being addicted is more than just a choice. It's a disease. Because I'm an addict, if I jump off a bridge, I'm going to do it again. The adrenaline. The excitement of it. Walking on the waters of the unknown. I enjoy that.

When I went to meetings, I never tried to talk. I understood their language, but I didn't speak it myself. Some things I just wouldn't do. One woman asked me how I felt about coloring. What? I'm not going to lie on my stomach and color no damn picture! You're going to tell me it's therapeutic. I'm not doubting that. But that prescription does not meet my needs. When I say hey, listen, I'm not into coloring, I shouldn't be considered delinquent.

They worked me at fifty or sixty hours a week. Then they told me to go to meetings. In return, they gave me sixty-five dollars at the end of the week. That's no different from prison: one dollar an hour. I've seen that before. I can't help but think there's the same motives behind it.

I had to quit Wayside. I was there for too many months. And I didn't come up there to work. I came to get healed. I came to learn. There was another reason why I had to leave. The building I was staying in there used to be an old folks' home. There was a lot of mold. I went to the doctor because I was having respiratory problems, and he told me, you can't get healthy in that building. You just can't. And the people who owned the building and the people who ran the program knew about the mold before I knew it. But it didn't affect them. They were coming in and out. I was stuck there.

When you break into a place, the first thing you need to do is find another exit. If you came in through a window, you need to find another way out other than that window. When I went to Kentucky for sober living, I knew I had to find a way to escape if push came to shove. If other people are in control of you, then they can say leave at any time. And I'm in Kentucky with luggage. They could force me into compliance if I didn't have a way out. It's the same concept as a penitentiary. There's nothing set up there for you to get to your next chapter in life. And I recognized that. They practice dependency there. They'll say: "You can't make it out there! So-and-so went out there, and he's dead now!" Well, it's not because he left, it's because he chose not to use what he learned in recovery to make better decisions. That's what it is. I chose to go to Wayside. So, it was my choice to leave.

***

Now I am sitting in Omni, another sober living house in Louisville. I share the space with about nine other men. Each day, we have what is called morning meditation. Someone reads insightful thoughts from a daily meditation book. After the reading, hands go up one by one. Each man explains how those positive words filter through their drug-induced experiences. I listen, and when the baton passes to me, I talk about my life's mishaps.

I have spent a considerable amount of time wallowing in my swampy self. But right now, I'd like to step out of that and focus on the moments in my life when I knew I was fulfilling my divine purpose. Yes, I have been to swampy prisons. Yes, I have yoked myself to swampy people. But for every negative moment I've lived, there has been a plethora of memorable, positive ones.

One thought after another comes racing toward my pen, bullying me to write and express it first. *Writing Our Way Out* gave us, a collective group of coauthors, opportunities to stand on stages behind podiums and relay that one can change one's reality. The book opened doors to important rooms and people. But we were not just *in* those rooms, like silent pictures hanging on the wall, listening but never daring to speak. Hell no! We *worked* the rooms with precision, networking, spreading our gifts. Being in rooms with leaders, governors, mayors, the commonwealth's attorney—I did not feel outclassed at all. What a contrast to Greensville Correctional Center those rooms of prominence were, filled with suits and ties and cunning smiles. What a contrast to razor wires and bars.

In those events, my higher vibration self was in attendance. But as always, in the shadow of my higher vibration was my lower vibration, the part of me that loves bondage and captivity. My higher vibration self enjoyed the kinetic energy, moving around the room as we read from the book. But after those events, my low self would drive me home to my old reality of people, places, and things. People with addiction issues. Rooms for rent. Subsidized housing. Places of loneliness, isolation, and despair. Things I had grown accustomed to in and out of confinement. This duality is perplexing—to have one body with two selves, sometimes operating in harmony, but more often in opposition. I wonder, have I even forgiven myself for being myself?

* * *

When Andre, my brother from *Writing Our Way Out*, got himself killed, it was because he chose to do positive things during the day and negative things at night. I'm telling the same story as his actions. That's the duality of who we are as people.

This was my duality. *Writing Our Way Out* helped me grow. I could see the progress. It was like a spearhead, like the way Marines advance. They float up on the beach. There are battles. And every battle they win goes behind them until they now control that whole area. Every step out of prison has been a battle for me. Some battles have lasted longer than others. I battled my criminal mindset for years.

What saved me was that I enjoyed doing right more than doing wrong. My heart would hurt when I did wrong. It bothered me that I did Thrasher that way at The Local. It bothered me that I did Ben that way at Stockpile. When I caught that violation and that bullshit over the TV I stole—where I was dead wrong, where I went to the people's house and knocked at the door and said, Hey, listen, I didn't mean for it to turn out this way—I knew I needed to find my way back to my higher vibration.

I knew then that I could do right. Or I can do wrong. Today, I choose to do right.

Epilogue

Summer, 2025. A year after *Writing Our Way Out* was published, one of my students from VCU asked if she could adapt the book into a play. I gave her permission. She assembled the cast. At the end of the semester, the show opened.

It was compelling to hear the stories out loud in the actors' voices. The guy who played Dean had that same big-hearted smile and swagger. The guy who played Naji bore little resemblance to him physically, but he interpreted Naji's story with the same quiet intensity and precision. The one playing Andre read the scene where the police chased him and his associates over the Manchester Bridge until the car crashed, and the others fled. When he held up his hands and shouted to the police—"I was just a passenger! I don't know nothing!"—I experienced the same pang of fear I felt ten years ago when Andre read that story in jail.

But the feeling that lingered for days after the performance came from watching the actor playing Coogan. That was the name they used, instead of Dave, because the one playing me was a woman. There have been times when I wondered if my nurturing, listening, nonjudgmental nature was rooted in something more feminine than masculine. I no longer had to wonder as I watched this woman moving about the stage, eliciting the guys' stories, asking them questions, reflecting back their answers, and tending the space with insight and empathy.

I took a good look at Coogan. Not the actor playing me, but the man I had become in the years after that first writing class at the jail. In the jail classroom, I saw myself head-on. I knew what to do and who I was. After jail was like seeing myself in a dressing room three-way mirror. I was unfamiliar with these views of myself from the back or the side, revealing me as a witness, resource, ally, and mentor.

I had to learn how to see myself in new ways. Like the actors onstage that night, I had to make these roles mine. The guys have all gone through something similar after jail. They have taken up new roles as authors, public speakers, parents, entrepreneurs, community leaders, coaches, and volunteers. It took some time for them to make these roles theirs. None of them has gone back to prison. And the ones who returned to jail did not stay long. They got out, pushed their boats across the sand and into the sea of life, sat in the hull, gripped their oars, and began rowing toward the horizon of freedom.

Notes

1. Robin Schwartzkopf, "The History of Cobblestone Streets in Shockoe Slip," *RIC Today*, September 23, 2021, https://rictoday.6amcity.com/history-cobblestone-streets-shockoe-slip-richmond-va.
2. Elvatrice Belsches, "When Freedom Came," *Richmond Free Press*, April 9, 2015, https://richmondfreepress.com/news/2015/apr/09/when-freedom-came-part-3/.
3. Benjamin Campbell, *Richmond's Unhealed History* (Brandylane Publishers, 2012), 132, 157.
4. John O'Connor, "Timeline: The Quest to Replace the Diamond," *Richmond Times-Dispatch*, April 14, 2023, https://richmond.com/sports/flying-squirrels/timeline-the-quest-to-replace-the-diamond/article_ddd974be-dad2-11ed-b472-db4bac864b27.html.
5. Christina Sharpe, *In the Wake: On Blackness and Being* (Duke University Press, 2016), 22.
6. Campbell, *Richmond's Unhealed History*, 132, 157.
7. Michael Long, *Peaceful Neighbor: Discovering the Countercultural Mister Rogers* (Westminster John Knox Press, 2015); Shea Tuttle, *Exactly as You Are: The Life and Faith of Mister Rogers* (William B. Eerdmans Publishing Company, 2019).
8. *Mister Rogers' Neighborhood*, episode 1065, May 9, 1969, http://www.neighborhoodarchive.com/mrn/episodes/1065/index.html.
9. "The Legend of the Ducks," The Peabody Memphis, https://www.peabodymemphis.com/peabody-ducks.
10. Ronda Rich, "MLK and a Twist of Fate," *Gwinnett Daily Post*, July 7, 2018, https://www.gwinnettdailypost.com/opinion/columnists/rich-mlk-and-a-twist-of-fate/article_241bfb36-e98d-5b16-be87-c3ab4140c1b2.html.

11. Martin Luther King Jr., "The Three Evils of Society" (address delivered at the National Conference on New Politics, Chicago, IL, August 31, 1967), https://www.blackagendareport.com/speech-three-evils-society-martin-luther-king-jr-1967.
12. Bill Preston, "1968 Civil Rights Movement in Memphis," *The Tennessean*, Feb 24, 2018, https://www.tennessean.com/picture-gallery/news/2014/02/24/1968-civil-rights-movement-in-memphis/5775743/.
13. "The Peabody Hotel," Historic Memphis, https://historic-memphis.com/memphis-historic/peabody/peabody.html.
14. "Tennessee: The Lorraine Motel," The National Park Service, updated June 18, 2020, https://www.nps.gov/places/tennessee-the-lorraine-hotel-memphis.htm.
15. David Smith, "'Memphis Died with Dr King' – Shadow of Civil Rights Leader Haunts City," *The Guardian*, April 1, 2018, https://www.theguardian.com/us-news/2018/apr/01/martin-luther-king-memphis-mlk-50th-anniversary-death-lorraine-motel.
16. Greg Boyle, *Kinship and Kingdom*, from The Work of the People, https://www.theworkofthepeople.com/kinship-and-kingdom.
17. Bill W., *Alcoholics Anonymous: The Big Book*, 4th ed. (Alcoholics Anonymous World Services, 2001), 101, https://www.aa.org/sites/default/files/2021-11/en_bigbook_chapt7.pdf.
18. Bill McKelway and Reed Williams, "Man Killed in Police Chase Was a Longtime Felon – and Guest Lecturer at VCU," *Richmond Times-Dispatch*, December 8, 2009, https://richmond.com/news/man-killed-in-police-chase-was-a-longtime-felon----and-guest-lecturer/article_7d1ae8d2-5e97-5520-8c9b-1874e1d8f845.html.
19. Mary Oliver, *The Summer Day*, https://www.loc.gov/programs/poetry-and-literature/poet-laureate/poet-laureate-projects/poetry-180/all-poems/item/poetry-180-133/the-summer-day/.
20. Jennifer Thompson-Cannino and Ronald Cotton, *Picking Cotton: Our Story of Injustice and Redemption*, with Erin Torneo (St. Martin's Press, 2010).
21. Peter Matthiessen, *The Snow Leopard* (Penguin Books, 1978), 10.
22. Matthiessen, *The Snow Leopard*, 15.
23. Pablo Neruda, "The Builder," in *Fully Empowered* (New Directions, 1995).

24. Jean Giono, *The Man Who Planted Trees* (Shambhala, 2000).
25. Erik Erikson, "Insight and Responsibility," in *The Erik Erikson Reader*, ed. Robert Coles (Norton, 2000), 203–04.
26. Paul Eakin, *How Our Lives Become Stories: Making Selves* (Cornell University Press, 1999), x, 98.
27. "Baptist Meeting Bars Joint Move: Southern Body Reasserts Conservative Tradition," *New York Times*, May 21, 1964, https://www.nytimes.com/1964/05/21/archives/baptist-meeting-bars-joint-move-southern-body-reasserts.html.
28. Charles Marsh, *God's Long Summer: Stories of Faith and Civil Rights* (Princeton University Press, 2019).
29. James Baldwin, "On Being White and Other Lies," in *Black on White: Black Writers on What It Means to Be White*, ed. David Roediger (Schocken Books, 1998), 178–180.
30. Angela Duckworth, *Grit: The Power of Passion and Perseverance* (Scribner, 2016), 42.
31. David Denby, "The Limits of 'Grit,'" *The New Yorker*, June 21, 2016, https://www.newyorker.com/culture/culture-desk/the-limits-of-grit.
32. Duckworth, *Grit*, 283.
33. Roger Luckhurst, *The Trauma Question* (Routledge, 2008), 118–119.
34. Leon Festinger, *A Theory of Cognitive Dissonance* (Stanford University Press, 1957), 21–31.
35. "Where marijuana is legal in the United States," MJBizDaily, mjbizdaily.com/map-of-us-marijuana-legalization-by-state/.
36. Heather Cabot, *The New Chardonnay: The Unlikely Story of How Marijuana Went Mainstream* (Crown, 2020).
37. T. C. Brock and J. L. Balloun, "Behavioral Receptivity to Dissonant Information," *Journal of Personality and Social Psychology*, no. 6 (1967): 413–428, http://dx.doi.org/10.1037/h0021225; Eddie Harmon-Jones and Cindy Harmon-Jones, *Cognitive Dissonance: Reexamining a Pivotal Theory in Psychology* (American Psychological Association, 2019).
38. Bryan Stevenson, *Just Mercy: A Story of Justice and Redemption* (Spiegel & Grau, 2015).
39. Daniel J. Freed, "The Nonsystem of Criminal Justice," in *Law and Order Reconsidered: Report of the Task Force on Law and Law Enforcement*

to the National Commission on the Causes and Prevention of Violence, by James S. Campbell, Joseph R. Sahid, and David P. Stang (1969).

40. Neil Lewis, "Daniel J. Freed Dies at 82; Shaped Sentencing in U.S.," *New York Times*, January 22, 2010, https://www.nytimes.com/2010/01/22/us/22freed.html.
41. James Forman Jr., *Locking Up Our Own: Crime and Punishment in Black America* (Farrar, Straus, and Giroux, 2017).
42. Max Weber, "The Ethos of Office," in *Max Weber: Readings and Commentary on Modernity*, ed. Stephen Kalberg (Blackwell Publishing, 2005), 200–204.
43. Malcolm Bull, *On Mercy* (Princeton University Press, 2019), 141.
44. Claudia Card, "On Mercy," *The Philosophical Review* 81, no. 2 (1972): 182–207.
45. Forman, *Locking Up Our Own*, 147–148.
46. Erving Goffman, *The Presentation of Self in Everyday Life* (Doubleday, 1959), 10–13.
47. Liam Martin, "'Free but Still Walking the Yard': Prisonization and the Problems of Reentry," *Journal of Contemporary Ethnography* 47, no. 5 (2018): 671–694.
48. Goffman, *The Presentation of Self*, 81.
49. Goffman, *The Presentation of Self*, 59.

www.ingramcontent.com/pod-product-compliance
Lightning Source LLC
LaVergne TN
LVHW091145080826
845145LV00008B/2269

* 9 7 8 1 9 6 6 3 6 9 0 5 9 *